D1570680

NELSON'S CHURCH LEADER'S MANUAL

Morris Proctor and
Joshua D. Rowe,
General Editors

THOMAS NELSON
Since 1798

NASHVILLE   DALLAS   MEXICO CITY   RIO DE JANEIRO

Published in Nashville, Tennessee, by Thomas Nelson. Thomas Nelson is a trademark of Thomas Nelson, Inc.

Book design and composition by Upper Case Textual Services, Lawrence, Massachusetts.

Thomas Nelson, Inc., titles may be purchased in bulk for educational, business, fund-raising, or sales promotional use. For information, please e-mail SpecialMarkets@ThomasNelson.com.

Unless otherwise noted, Scripture quotations are taken from the KING JAMES VERSION of the Bible.

Scripture quotations marked NKJV are from the NEW KING JAMES VERSION. © 1982 by Thomas Nelson, Inc. Used by permission. All rights reserved.

Scripture quotations marked NASB are from the NEW AMERICAN STANDARD BIBLE®. © The Lockman Foundation 1960, 1962, 1963, 1968, 1971, 1972, 1973, 1975, 1977. Used by permission.

Library of Congress Cataloging-in-Publication Data
978-1-4185-4360-0 Hardcover

Printed in the United States of America

1 2 3 4 5 6 RRD 13 12 11 10

Table of Contents

Contributors v

Part One: Preparation
Be spiritually and mentally prepared for leadership.
- Leading Through Serving. 3
- Cultivating Spiritual Maturity 9
- Nurturing Creativity. 17

Part Two: Organization
Structure your approach to ministry.
- "GO" Stands for Get Organized 25
- Time Management 33
- Working with Busy Pastors and
  Church Staff 39
- Strategic Planning 47
- Planning with Perspective 57
- Setting Policies. 65

Part Three: Relationships
Know how to work with people.
- Unity and Diversity 77
- The Purpose and Planning of
  Leadership Retreats 83
- Recruiting Volunteers 91
- Identifying and Implementing
  Spiritual Gifts 97
- Learning to Listen 105
- Preparing Members for Change 111
- Mentoring and Discipleship 119

Part Four: Strategy

Carry a big toolbox.

- Live and Teach the Gospel 129
- Leading a Small-Group Bible Study 133
- Preservice/In-Service Training 143
- Technology and Ministry 153
- How to Lead an Effective Meeting 159
- Tools of the Trade 167
- Setting and Enforcing Budgets 175
- Liability and Security Issues in Ministry . . . 181

Part Five: Problem Solving

Expect problems and be prepared.

- A Biblical Perspective on Problems 193
- Damage Control and Prevention 201
- Dealing with Difficult Members 211
- Removing Ineffective Leaders Without
  Losing Them 219
- Integrating New People into
  Existing Groups 227
- Flexibility in Ministry 235

Part Six: Motivation

Keep going.

- Dealing with Burnout 243
- Passion and Enthusiasm 251
- Perseverance 257
- Encouragement and Affirmation 263

Endotes 269

Contributors

Lisa Baker
PLACE ministry coordinator for Brentwood Baptist Church, Brentwood, TN

Identifying and Implementing Spiritual Gifts

Dr. Doug Dees
Associate pastor of education at Henderson Hills Baptist Church in Edmond, OK, and president of Releasing Churches, Inc., a nonprofit group "helping good churches get better"

Unity and Diversity
Flexibility in Ministry

Neil Glotfelty
Director of information systems with the Association of Baptists for World Evangelism

Technology and Ministry

Dr. Craig A. Green
Pastor of First United Methodist Church, Livingston, TN

Removing Ineffective Leaders Without Losing Them

Stephen Helm
Executive pastor of The People's Church, Franklin, TN

Setting Policies

Steffron T. James
Pastor of Kingdom Living Ministries in Murfreesboro, TN

Mentoring and Discipleship

Kurt Jenkins
Pastor of serving, Central Assembly of God, Houston, PA

Integrating New People into Existing Groups
Organizing Church Functions
Planning with Perspective

Ed Jent
Associate pastor/minister of education, Eastwood Baptist
Church, Bowling Green, KY

Working with Busy Pastors and Church Staff
How to Lead an Effective Meeting

Ron Kairdolf
Pastor of Christian Life Church of Murfreesboro, TN

Damage Control and Prevention

Dr. Earl B. Mason
Pastor of Bible-Based Fellowship Church of Temple
Terrace in Tampa, FL

The Purpose and Planning of Leadership Retreats

Debra Moore
President of Moore Educational Publishers in Nashville, TN

Leading a Small-Group Bible Study

Robert J. Morgan
Senior pastor of The Donelson Fellowship in Nashville, TN

> Nurturing Creativity
> "GO" Stands for Get Organized
> Time Management

Jeff Nichols
Executive pastor of The Donelson Fellowship in Nashville, TN

> Tools of the Trade: Organizational Charts,
> Ministry Descriptions, and Yearly Goals

Randal D. Ongie
Former executive pastor for thirteen years, currently Project Consultant serving churches with Cogun, Inc.

> Strategic Planning
> Setting and Enforcing Budgets

Dr. Rusty Ricketson
Associate professor of leadership, Luther Rice Seminary and University

> Leading Through Serving

Dr. Kevin Riggs
Founder and pastor of Franklin Community Church and author of *Failing Like Jesus*.

> Dealing with Burnout

Bob R. Roberts
Director of Kids 4 Truth International

>   Liability and Security Issues in Ministry

Kevin R. Scruggs
Pastor of marriage and family at First Baptist Church in Elk Grove, CA

>   Recruiting Volunteers
>   Passion and Enthusiasm
>   Encouragement and Affirmation

Yvonne Thigpen
President, Evangelical Training Association

>   PreService/In-Service Training

Monty Waldron
Church planter and pastor of Fellowship Bible Church of Rutherford County in Murfreesboro, TN

>   Learning to Listen
>   Preparing Members for Change
>   Dealing with Difficult Members
>   Perseverance

Wally Weaver
Elder and congregational care pastor of Henderson Hills Baptist Church in Edmond, OK

>   A Biblical Perspective on Problems

Dr. Donald S. Whitney
Associate professor of biblical spirituality (2005); senior associate dean of the School of Theology, The Southern Baptist Theological Seminary in Louisville, KY

Cultivating Spiritual Maturity

Special thanks to Stephen L. Fox of Clearly Media (www.clearlymedia.com) for his assistance with graphic illustration.

Part One
Preparation

Leading Through Serving
Dr. Rusty Ricketson

Anyone who has been a church leader for any length of time has experienced the joys and delights as well as the struggles and disappointments of working with others to achieve kingdom goals. I vividly remember my first pastorate as a place where fantasy met reality for this young, newly minted seminary graduate. After ministering in a new church start for several months, it became apparent that the pews the church had purchased from another church were not flexible enough to meet the ever-changing need for space as attendance increased. I thought it prudent for the church to purchase stackable chairs so that the space we used for worship could be used for other purposes during the weekdays. After several months of praying and talking, the church reluctantly agreed. We gave the pews to another church, bought the stackable chairs, and the church continued to grow.

In my fifth year of ministry, another church plant contacted me about becoming their pastor, so my family and I moved to a new town and new work. Several years after the move, I was in the town where my first church was located; I decided to drop by and see how they were doing. No one was around when I arrived, so I took the opportunity to look through a window. What I saw both shocked and bemused me. There, where the stackable chairs used to be, were row upon row of pews.

I then realized that all the supposed change I had led the church to make in order to position the church for growth was not really change at all. I had simply succeeded in rearranging the furniture for a few years.

As leaders we pray for God's wisdom, seek wise counsel, listen to input from others, and read every piece of material available in order to make the best decisions for our particular congregations or ministries. Change is usually a difficult process, and sometimes the pressures of ministry can be so overwhelming we find ourselves crying out, "Lord, what am I doing here?" As a leader, the answer to this question is crucial to a continuing, productive ministry.

Follow the Will of the Father

Looking at the life of Jesus, it is clear He knew why He was here on planet earth. Jesus said, "For I came down from heaven, not to do mine own will, but the will of him that sent me" (John 6:38). Jesus' purpose was simple and direct. He was to follow the will of the Father. Jesus was the best leader who ever lived because His first priority, His ultimate purpose, was to be the best follower who ever lived.[1] In fact, when we look in the Bible for direct teaching from Jesus on being a leader, the Bible is unusually silent. What we find instead is Jesus saying, "Neither be ye called masters: for one is your Master, even Christ" (Matt. 23:10). Other translations of this verse translate the word for "master" as teacher or leader. Regardless of how the word is translated, the context of the passage indicates that Jesus' primary teaching is not so much on the title a person holds as the attitude a person has.

Our first calling is a call to follow Christ. As born-again believers, we revel in the fact that Christ calls us His followers. As we follow Christ, the Lord blesses us with a second call to be responsible for equipping others to follow Christ (Eph. 4:11). Although Christ calls us His followers, those over whom we have responsibility will call us leaders. Leading others in any capacity comes with an inherent temptation, even more so in the church. What we must guard against is the temptation of giving more credence to what the people call us rather than what Christ calls us.

Serve the Lord Jesus Christ

In John 12:26, Jesus said, "If any man serve me, let him follow me; and where I am, there shall also my servant be: if any man serve me, him will my Father honour." Our first role in the kingdom is to be servants to the Lord Jesus Christ. A seasoned pastor once shared with me that if I were to take on the role of a minister, my primary role would be to serve Jesus first and the people second. As leaders we know all too well how the cries for help and the looming needs of a hurting congregation can drown out the still small voice of the Holy Spirit inviting us to times of intimacy with the Savior. We know what it is to be tempted to compromise biblical principle in order to pacify the perceived needs of the people. However, by understanding our role as a servant to the Lord Jesus, the needs of the people and pressures of ministry find their rightful place.

Additionally, the Lord Jesus promises that God will honor that one who follows and serves Him. With a servant's heart we can concentrate on serving the Lord and not become sidetracked by concerns for the size and scope of "our" ministries. In fact, a servant's heart changes our terminology altogether. Instead of being "our" ministries, we understand more clearly that all we do is "His" ministry. Whether Jesus asks us to serve before thousands or to be faithful with a few, our focus is always the same. As Jesus instructed in Luke 17:10, "So likewise ye, when ye shall have done all those things which are commanded you, say, We are unprofitable servants: we have done that which was our duty to do."

Lead Others to Follow the Savior

A biblical leader follows the will of the Father, serves the Lord Jesus Christ first, and then leads others to follow Him. This is the essence of the command in the Great Commission to "make disciples" (Matt. 28:18–20 NKJV). By understanding our role as servants, we are enabled by the Holy Spirit to assume the responsibility of leading others through manifesting the same servant-leader style employed by the Savior. It is not coincidental that the Lord follows His teaching on position and title with these words: "But he that is greatest among you shall be your servant" (Matt. 23:11).

Following the will of the Father by being a servant to others resonates throughout the life of the Savior. On one occasion, when the disciples became angry because two of their group had the audacity to ask to sit on Jesus' right and left hand in the kingdom, Jesus responded with these words:

> Ye know that the princes of the Gentiles exercise dominion over them, and they that are great exercise authority upon them. But it shall not be so among you: but whosoever will be great among you, let him be your minister; And whosoever will be chief among you, let him be your servant: Even as the Son of man came not to be ministered unto, but to minister, and to give his life a ransom for many. (Matt. 20:25–28)

Again we see the Savior pointing out the difference between the world's idea of leading and God's idea of assuming the servant's role when leading others. The world's methodology for leading is through power and control. God's methodology for leading is through submission and responsibility.[2] We submit to the Lord as our ultimate leader and fulfill our responsibility as outlined in the Bible. The Lord Jesus exemplifies this role through countless acts of obedience, kindness, and service. What we learn from Jesus' life is that the most menial and seemingly routine behaviors take on extraordinary eternal value when performed in service to God.

Jesus listened with understanding to the common man and woman. Jesus observed needs and had compassion on both the wealthy and the poor. Jesus loved and gave Himself, even to those who stood against Him. He found ways to serve His family, friends, and strangers.

It is humbling to see the King of kings take the servant's role and gird a towel about His waist and wash the disciples' feet (John 13:3–5). It is overwhelming to witness the selflessness of the Savior as He prays "not my will, but thine, be done" (Luke 22:42). Yet His life is consistent with His teaching in that Jesus said, "If any man will come after me, let him deny himself, and take up his cross daily, and follow me" (Luke 9:23). As ministers of the gospel called to lead His church, let us always live with Christ's same purpose, serve Him as preeminent in all things, and lead His people with His same heart: the heart of a servant.

Cultivating Spiritual Maturity
Are the Christian Spiritual Disciplines Increasingly Important to You?
Dr. Donald S. Whitney

When we got a wood-burning stove I learned what it means to build a fire. The first flash of match and paper is bright and impressive, but the reason I build the fire is to enjoy the sustained heat of burning logs and slow-glowing coals.

Perhaps you are like a Christian I know who sometimes wonders if she is still growing spiritually because the original, God-kindled blaze of eternal life, which once illuminated the darkness of her life so suddenly, seldom flames up as dramatically as when she was first converted. But what is true for the woodstove is true in this case for the Christian heart as well—just because the beginning of the combustion may briefly be more spectacular than at present does not mean the fire is not growing. The initial burst of spiritual flame may be more dazzling, but heartfire's greatest effectiveness occurs as it burns into consistency.

Nothing contributes to the growth of spiritual heat and light more than the persevering practice of the Christian spiritual disciplines. These disciplines are the bellows and iron poker, tools in God's hands through which He stokes and blows upon the eternal fire He Himself ignites in His people.

What Are the Spiritual Disciplines?

The Christian spiritual disciplines are the God-ordained means by which we bring ourselves before God, experience Him, and are changed into Christlikeness. The Lord is omnipresent and we often encounter Him in unexpected places and surprising ways. Nevertheless, it has pleased Him to establish specific means—the spiritual disciplines—whereby we may expect to encounter Him regularly and be transformed by Him.

These devotional and sanctifying practices have been categorized in many ways. One approach classifies them as personal and interpersonal disciplines, meaning some disciplines are practiced in isolation, others in community. Examples of the former are the private reading of and meditating on Scripture, individual prayer, fasting, solitude, and keeping a spiritual journal. Disciplines that require the presence of others include congregational worship, corporate prayer, the Lord's Supper, and fellowship. Many of the disciplines taught in the Bible can be practiced both alone and with the church. For instance, we can study the Bible either on our own or with a group, or both.[3]

Keep in mind that the spiritual disciplines are biblical, that is, God-given and found in His written Word. Whatever might be said about them, those practices originating from ourselves, derived from the culture, or discovered in other religions may not properly be considered Christian spiritual disciplines.

Remember also that the spiritual disciplines found in Christian Scripture are sufficient. God has revealed in the pages of the Bible every devotional and transformational practice necessary. No other ceremony, rite, ritual, religious habit, or spiritual exercise is needed for progress in Christlikeness.

Moreover, the Spirit of God works through each of these disciplines in unique ways. What He gives through one discipline He does not duplicate in another. You cannot receive through a prayer meeting the identical blessings given through fasting, and vice versa. All the Christian spiritual disciplines are important and singularly beneficial.

Recognize, too, that the spiritual disciplines are practices, not attitudes. Do not confuse them with character qualities, Christian graces, or "the fruit of the Spirit" (Gal. 5:22–23). Prayer is a spiritual discipline; love—strictly speaking—is not. Although we must never separate the external practices known as the spiritual disciplines from the internal realities that are their impulse and power, we may distinguish them.

Why Should I Practice the Spiritual Disciplines?

We are exhorted in Hebrews 12:14 to "follow … holiness, without which no man shall see the Lord." Following holiness is not what qualifies us to "see the Lord"; it is the Lord Himself who qualifies us for this by grace through faith in the life and death of Jesus Christ. Rather, the ongoing pursuit of holiness (i.e., sanctification, godliness, Christlikeness) is characteristic of everyone who is on the way to "see the Lord" in heaven.

If no one will go to heaven without pursuing holiness/Christlikeness/godliness, then it is crucial to ask, "How do we pursue it?"

"Discipline yourself," answers 1 Timothy 4:7 (NASB), "for the purpose of godliness." And the way to "discipline yourself" is to engage in the disciplines commanded and modeled in the Bible. In short, the Christian spiritual disciplines are the means to godliness, to the "holiness, without which no man shall see the Lord."

Are the Christian spiritual disciplines increasingly important to you? Of course, it is not necessarily a mark of growth when the disciplines take a greater percentage of your daily/weekly time than they used to (though that might be very significant). What does matter is whether their influence continues to expand in your life. Growing Christians have a growing appetite for those things that bring the sweetest enjoyment of God.

Engaging in the Christian disciplines is much more than imitating Jesus' example, however. The spiritual disciplines are the biblical avenues of intentional communion with Christ by those who love Him. As you grow closer to Jesus, you will obviously gravitate toward the means of that intimacy. You will not think of the disciplines as mere duty, nor simply as Christlike patterns to follow, but rather as life and light from heaven to your soul.

What Are the Dangers of the Disciplines?

The mere rise of the disciplines in your priorities does not necessarily indicate a rise in your likeness to Christ. It is possible to be exemplary in discipline, but this must be accompanied by faith and love of God. Apart from the presence and sanctifying work of the Holy Spirit within, empty practices of discipline only render a person even more culpable at the Judgment.

So the spiritual disciplines are not by themselves the marks of Christlikeness as much as they are the means to it. Without understanding this distinction, it is possible for someone to practice the disciplines and be far from Christ. Even true believers can spend hours each week in the disciplines and not grow spiritually if their motive is misplaced or if they equate bare devotional activity with godliness. Only God's grace working through the disciplines can transform those who practice them with the eyes of faith on Him.

Besides a wrongly motivated usage of the disciplines, another danger is imbalance. Strangely, some of those Christians most active in church are most in need of examining their relationship to the disciplines. Remember that we are called to engage in both corporate and personal spiritual disciplines. Many believers enthusiastically engage in the corporate disciplines, leaving little time to practice the personal ones. Or perhaps they content themselves with the thought that extraordinary involvement in the interpersonal disciplines excuses them from the personal disciplines. Or they think, "I'm always at church; why do I need to practice those personal disciplines?"

Serving in the church is a virtue—needed by churches today more than ever. But some who serve so faithfully have no time for prayer or meditation on Scripture, the two most important personal disciplines. Working for Christ is right; it is healthy Christianity. But working for Christ in a way that leaves insufficient time to be alone with Christ and His Word is spiritually unhealthy and wrong. As much as Jesus gave Himself to the daily service of the Father, He did not neglect the refreshment of His own soul through regular communion with the Father through the personal spiritual disciplines. (For examples, see Matt. 14:23; Mark 1:35; and Luke 4:42).

At the other extreme, those submerged in their own private "spirituality" need the balance of the corporate disciplines. While God-centered solitude and the other personal spiritual disciplines are essential for growth in Christlikeness, so are public worship and prayer, fellowship, service to and with other believers, the hearing of God's Word preached, and the communion of saints around the Lord's Supper, just as we find in the practice of Christ's people in the New Testament. Any who think it pleases God for them to seek Him in private while rejecting His people are greatly mistaken.

What Should I Do?

In one sense I have answered that question with book-length responses elsewhere. (See note 3 again.)

Let me here make three suggestions that are always appropriate.

Devote yourself more to the pursuit of Christlikeness and the enjoyment of God through the spiritual disciplines than to the pursuit of efficiency and the completion of to-do lists. The increasing pace of life and the inexorable roll of "progress" in our culture foster neither the growth of the soul nor the improvement of relationships, either with God or others (including family, fellow believers, and the lost). What good is our multitasking, the accomplishment of more and more, and the acquisition of wealth, if we are not—by the means God has given us—becoming more like Jesus, the One we live for, the One who will evaluate our lives?

Resist the temptation to believe in microwave spirituality or shortcut Christlikeness. One thing that will always be an exception to acceleration is the rate of growth in godliness. The increasing speed of our machines cannot stimulate a corresponding rate in the growth of our souls. Faster Internet connections do not make us like Jesus more quickly. But whatever time and effort is required, the pursuit of intimacy with and likeness to Jesus Christ is worth it all.

Stoke your spiritual life with at least one perceptible poke. When a well-wooded fire in my stove burns low, usually a good nudge or two with the iron poker restores its vitality. Having now invested part of your life to read this chapter, do not turn from it without choosing at least one sharp spiritual discipline to make at least one noticeable nudge in the fire of your soul's growth.

Nurturing Creativity
Robert J. Morgan

For a long time, I did not consider myself creative. The very term intimidated me. I am a traditional guy at heart, a little staid and stuffy. I do not bungee jump or wear tie-dye. I prefer Bach to rock. I enjoy the Doxology on the Lord's Day, and we still have Sunday night services.

But I was not always that way. As a child, my imagination resembled a kitten in a room of wind-up toys. I chased every idea, scratched every itch, and pounced on every adventure. My secondhand bicycle became alternately a helicopter and a powerboat. I unraveled mysteries and swept starlets off their feet. I composed poems and plays.

When I lurched into adolescence, my imagination followed like a shadow. It questioned boring traditions, dreaming of better ways and better days. It wondered why no one had ever done a thousand doable things. But twenty years later I did not consider myself an innovator. Why? What happened between adolescence and adulthood to silence my imagination?

"I Think I Can't, I Think I Can't"

Lack of self-confidence is the biggest barrier to creativity. We become set in our ways, afraid to change, too old to dream—or so we think.

The acceleration of change in our society makes creativity increasingly important. The ancient message requires up-to-date ways and means to stay relevant with contemporary culture. That is why many businesses now offer creativity training for their employees. That is why dozens of books, recordings, games, and software focus on creativity exercises and processes. That is why increasing numbers of universities offer degrees in creativity training.

I still appreciate the benefits of the traditional, but I do not want to be confined by its liabilities. I want to be "like unto a man that is an householder, which bringeth forth out of his treasure things new and old" (Matt. 13:52). God sowed the seeds of creativity in the furrows of the left side of my brain, and I realize now is the time to cultivate for the harvest.

So I made an irrevocable decision: to once again think of myself as an imagineer. I would guide my staff and church to dream.

I have learned to do that by keeping five steps in mind. I call them my M&Ms, and I use them to feed my imagination.

Milk

"I milk a lot of cows, but I churn my own butter," said one preacher. Original thinking is seldom original; it just looks that way.

I begin by milking all the ideas I can from others. I read, study, interview, inspect, dissect, and observe. I take classes and endure seminars. I subscribe and ascribe, describe and transcribe, gathering premium ideas wherever possible, for only God can make something from nothing.

Take existing ideas and play with them, turning them upside down and inside out. Challenge them, change them, and channel them in unlikely directions. Churn milk into butter, and then press it into different molds.

As a young pastor, my church was small enough to provide all of the pastoral care. As it grew, however, I read of a program developed by another denomination. I decided to import it into our church. The fanfare did not last long. Despite my good intentions, the ministry sputtered along and then fizzled. I learned the hard way you cannot take an idea and slap it up like a piece of wallpaper. You have to take a lot of ideas and mix them together like custom-colored paint.

Our leadership started reading everything we could about lay-pastoral programs. We attended "Equipping the Laity for Ministry"–type seminars. We visited churches, telephoned pastors, reviewed notebooks, and conducted surveys. We blended colors, used others as enamel highlights, and ended up with our own uniquely designed program. We commissioned our own lay pastors, who are now doing an admirable job.

Meet

Having milked all the available cows, the next step is to gather the butter-makers into one room for brainstorming, a time when we gather around the table with our pails of milk and start splashing one another. We suspend criticism and toss around ideas capriciously.

A great time for brainstorming is the beginning of leadership meetings, before we have exhausted our mental energies on calendars or budgets. As an example, a group of leaders in my congregation had a meeting to discuss a problem in the previous Sunday night's service. That night, we had placed a call to a missionary in France, but it did not channel through our audio system.

One leader suggested we pay the money to do these types of calls right. Another leader chimed in that the technology was simply too expensive. Yet another leader asked what other uses we might have for this technology. By the end of this idea-bouncing discussion, we had come up with a dozen possibilities and enough excitement to carry us through the rest of the meeting with enthusiasm.

Mist

There is a problem.

The brainstorming process usually ends in the fabulous frustration of too many ideas. We become too involved to be rational, too hot for cold calculation, too close for objective thinking. A thick mental mist descends.

Solo creative efforts such as sermon or lesson preparation also involve this stage of perplexity. After we have exegeted the text, read the commentaries, and gathered the data, the questions arise: Now what? What do I do with all this stuff? What direction do I take? It is like fighting through a corridor thick with cobwebs.

But, as a reborn imagineer, I eventually recognized this as a good sign. It means we are right in the middle of the creative process, on our way to the fourth phase.

Mull

For the creative, leisure is no luxury. Needing time and solitude, imagineers walk frequently around Walden Pond. They are children of Isaac who "went out to meditate in the field at the eventide" (Gen. 24:63). That is why creative people often appear absentminded.

I periodically go for a couple of days to a state park an hour's drive from my house that has cabins with cheap rent. I think of it as a Camp David—my version of the president's weekend stomping grounds. I retreat there to ponder and pray. Our church leaders often withdraw there annually for the same purpose. Ideas must incubate a while before they are hatched. They must wander through the chambers of the mind before they are ready for debut. That often happens as I wander through the forests of the Cumberland Mountains.

Failing that, a hammock in the backyard will do. Or a jog around the block. Or a bit of pacing in the family room. As I hike, sway, jog, or pace, I ask a lot of questions. I visualize. I throw words into the air and see how they land. I squeeze ideas like oranges to see if they render any juice. In a word, I mull.

The words *mull*, *mill*, and *meal* all come from an Old English root meaning the pulverizing of corn in a grinder. To mull over a subject is to ponder it, to pulverize it in the millstones of the mind.

Instant ideas are usually more futile then fertile, for "the prudent man looketh well to his going" (Prov. 14:15).

Map

After I have worked through the above steps, I usually get my hands on an idea or vision ready to be mapped out in action steps. Perhaps it is a sermon to be preached, a program to be implemented, a technique to try, or an innovation to launch. I have to take my big idea and do the hard work of working out the details of implementation.

Thousands of good ideas have never seen the light of day because the persons who conceived them did not have the ability to take what is in their heads and execute a plan. Like Joseph, the expert in dreams who also masterminded the administration of the huge Egyptian food plan, I have to be both a dreamer and a doer, an imagineer and an engineer.

There is a price to be paid for creativity. There will be changes and risks. As time goes by, implementing your ideas will require large doses of evaluation and correction. Many will be tried and discarded. But that is all right. Get ready. Let the imagineers return.

Part Two
Organization

"GO" Stands for Get Organized
Robert J. Morgan

I had a friend who organized his working life twice each year. I could tell what month it was by watching his office. It became more and more disastrous until it reached a certain critical mass. Then he would take several days to empty the room, hauling every knickknack, every book, every piece of clothing, and all furniture and equipment out into the hallway. He'd bring in a Dumpster and start going through things, throwing away half of it and carting the other half back into his office where he situated it in a pristine way. When he finished, his office looked like a picture from a magazine. But he did not have a system of regular maintenance, and so from the moment he reopened his office it started deteriorating until, six months later, he would have to go through the whole exhausting exercise again.

At least we can say he had the right initial idea. The first thing you have to do is get organized. It is important to set up receptacles so that everything has its logical place, along with setting up and implementing maintenance systems, flowcharts, planning calendars, filing cabinets, storage bins, and all the other time-tested tools of efficiency. You cannot work in self-induced chaos.

In the same way, our ministries need organization. It is tempting for church workers to fly by the seat of their pants. We like to think of our congregations in family terms, and rightfully so. But sometimes that causes us to resent and resist needed systems and processes in church life. While we have always got to keep our organizational systems as simple as possible, we need to think in terms of position descriptions, organizational charts, minimal guidelines, short-term goals, policy requirements, and standard operating procedures.

If you are only ministering to a dozen or so people, that is fine; you can get by with minimal planning and few systems. But once you start growing, as the apostles discovered in Acts 6, you have to create an organizational structure that will manage your numbers and expand with your growth.

A God of Order

Creating organization structure is what Moses did. When he led the children of Israel out of Egypt, they were a disorganized mass, without any structure of centralized leadership. The books of Exodus, Leviticus, and Numbers are a description of God's method of nation building. In Exodus 18, a judicial system was put into place. In the following chapters, laws were given to govern the civil operations of the nation. The last part of Exodus and all of Leviticus describe the setting up of worship patterns for the nation. In Numbers, an army was conscripted. The nation was divided into divisions, a census was taken, and the placement of the tribes around the Tabernacle was prescribed in exacting detail. Also in Numbers, the priests and their fellow officials were put into place. Then in the book of Deuteronomy, the up-and-coming generation was given its heritage in written form.

When the Israelites passed through the Red Sea they were a mass of people without laws, rules, governing structures, religious habits, or cultural mores. By the time they passed through the Jordan River to possess the land, they were a fully functioning and well-organized nation with national machinery and centralized operations.

I believe that is what God intends for our lives and ministries. He wants to bring order out of pandemonium, systems out of chaos, structure out of confusion, and organization out of disorder. Everything we can observe about God's personality and methods tells us this. Organization is built into the very fabric of this universe. The human cell is a genius of organization, and even the atom is perfectly designed. If you study the stellar heavens, there is organization there, and the laws of physics and mathematics operate consistently throughout the cosmos.

In the Bible, even the legions of heavenly angels are organized, and in the Old Testament so was the young Israelite nation as the tribes camped around the Tabernacle. Companies, corporations, and commercial enterprises need administrators who oversee effective sets of systems that keep the organization moving forward. In the church and home, the Bible provides an organizational structure that gives purpose, order, and arrangement. The reason the universe is well ordered and everything in the universe requires order is because of the nature of the Trinity. God Himself is organized in mysterious ways we can never fully understand.

The apostle Paul said, "God is not the author of confusion.... Let all things be done decently and in order" (1 Cor. 14:33, 40). In its immediate context, the writer was talking about church worship services, but the principle applies to all of church life.

Where to Begin

In your particular ministry, think through the purpose of your work. What do you want to accomplish in five years. That is your vision. What do you want to accomplish in one year? That is your goal. What do you want to accomplish in six months? That is your plan.

Whom do you need working with you and what do you want them to do? With whom do they work? To whom do they report? The answers to those questions provide your job (or ministry) description and your organizational chart.

The Lord does not need one-person bands—individuals going around with cymbals on their knees, drums around their waists, guitars across their chests, and a harmonica in their mouths. He wants us to recruit, train, empower, and organize others for the work. He wants an orchestra with everyone doing its part in coordinated harmony.

You seldom have to start from scratch. Churches and Christian organizations have been around long enough to have the organization part of it figured out. If your church has a vacation Bible school, for example, the training kits should come with all you need to recruit, train, and organize the workers. If your church participates in a national ministry or para-church work, those are often effectively organized; all you have to do is follow the plan.

But often we have to put on our thinking caps and devise some systems ourselves. Do not be afraid to do it, and do not fail to attempt it. Either you are a one-man band who will wear yourself out, or you will learn to bring systems into play that allow you to share your work with others, as Moses learned in Exodus 18 from Jethro.

The Master Leader

Jesus was a master at organizing and delegating. When He fed the 5,000, He had everyone sit down in organized groups of fifties and hundreds so the food could be distributed in an orderly and well-organized way. And after the meal, Jesus had the place cleaned up with all the leftovers going into baskets so that nothing would be wasted.

And if you want an enriching Bible study, read through the Gospels and notice how often He sent His workers to do His job for Him. He was a brilliant recruiter, trainer, and delegator. So effective was He that within three years, He was able to turn everything over to Peter, James, and John—and to you and me.

Jesus realized that not even He Himself could do everything. In Acts 10:38, the apostle Peter said of Jesus that He was anointed with the Holy Spirit and went around doing good. It does not say that He went around doing everything. Indeed, Jesus often left the scene while the work was seemingly unfinished. At the end of His three years of public ministry, only a portion of one tiny nation had been reached. The world was still filled with sick, lonely, dying people. His own homeland was dotted with towns and cities still untouched by His message.

But Jesus knew how to work Himself out of a job, so to speak. He was a master delegator, and He devoted much of His time preparing a handful of men to take over His work, and through them to continue the cause.

This was our Lord's strategy. He was always training others to do the work He had begun and assigning them the work they could do for Him or with Him. The one thing Jesus could not delegate was the Cross. No one else in heaven or on earth could die righteously for the sins of the world. Only He could do that. But as soon as He had accomplished that and had risen again, what did He do? He started commissioning all His followers again so they could take over the world.

You need to stop trying to do it all yourself. Ask yourself this basic question: "What are the things that I alone can do?" Then take everything else and begin to find ways of passing it along to someone else. That is not laziness. That is biblical wisdom, prudent decentralization, and ethical delegation.

At my church, we are trying our best to help our staff understand that their primary role is to be an overseer, not an implementer. In your workplace, try your best to work your way out of a job. If you are in a position of authority with people working under you, learn to train and entrust them with the work. Delegating our work does not mean we pass it along and then forget about it. We cannot just delegate it and dismiss it. We are still responsible for it, but we do it through others whom we oversee. As someone said once, "It's not what you expect but what you inspect that gets done." But people who try to work their way out of a job never fail to have a better one ahead of them.

Time Management
Robert J. Morgan

Until we appreciate the value of time and learn to manage it with skill, we cannot manage ourselves. But when we learn to manage our time, we will manage our lives. We will better handle our tasks and our daily work; and as we do so consistently we will lastly arrive at the end of life having accomplished the work Christ gave us to do.

This is stewardship. Usually in the Christian world, when we think of stewardship we think of money. But time is like currency of a different realm; it is the coinage of life. If we mismanage our money, we simply try to make more of it. But there is no way of making any more time. When a moment is gone, it is gone forever, like sand through an hourglass. We cannot rent, buy, steal, or borrow any more of it.

Ephesians 5:15–16 says, "See then that ye walk circumspectly, not as fools, but as wise, Redeeming the time, because the days are evil." It is imperative for us to wisely manage our life agendas and our daily schedules.

We have never been so hurried or worried. Somehow all our time-saving technology has made us busier than ever. Psychologists warn that humans are not equipped to process the vast amount of stimuli, the massive quantity of messages, and the expansive number of tasks that hit us every day. The sheer volume of everyday life is overwhelming our systems.

Prior to arriving as a student at Columbia International University, I'd never needed to worry much about clocks and calendars. I drifted through life without a keen sense of purpose or planning. My life was simple enough to keep it all in my mind—be at school every morning at 8:15, and do not forget Friday's ballgame. Now, all of a sudden, I had to juggle class schedules with study time and work hours. It quickly whirled into a sort of frantic agitation with missed deadlines, all-nighters, near misses, short tempers, and frenzied nerves.

After one particularly upsetting episode, I sat down at my desk with a piece of typing paper in the horizontal position, a ruler, a pen, and a set of colored pencils. Drawing six lines down the page, I created seven columns. I drew horizontal lines for the hours, and I managed to capture all the waking hours of the week within the parameters of an 8 1/2 by 11 1/2-inch page. Pulling out my colored pencils, I started blocking out the nonnegotiables, such as my class periods. With another color, I shaded in my work schedule. After all my set obligations were in place, I looked at all the white space that remained, and I chose some of it for study. In this way, I established regular study hours for the first time in my life. Friday night was colored in as an "evening off" to do whatever I wanted. And so forth.

I tacked my page to the wall by my desk and I lived by it faithfully. I learned that interruptions may disrupt my schedule, but they can be handled better within the framework of a schedule than outside of one.

That was forty years ago, and I am still doing the same thing. I no longer use rulers and colored pencils. I have an electronic calendar system on my computer and mobile phone, plus a monthly at-a-glance calendar in my notebook. But in essence, the procedure is the same.

It helps tremendously to provide a visual roadmap of our time—a daily, weekly, monthly, and annual calendar, putting in the scheduled items over which we have no control, inserting the important items in a deliberate way, and letting everything else take up the remainder.

The way to escape some of the burden of busyness is with the judicious use of a personal calendar. The secret is to get to the calendar before anyone else does. We have to block out time in our calendars in advance for the important, and then let pressing demands fill in the gaps. Most people do the opposite, resulting in the "tyranny of the urgent."

What is important in life? Time for prayer, Bible study, reading, thinking, and soul refreshment; time with our spouses; time with our children; time to rest; time working on those major projects that will establish our legacies. Each morning as we review our calendars, we simply have to make sure those items are in place before the rush of the day floods our schedules. Block off time for the truly important, and learn to control your schedule instead of letting your schedule control you.

Marriage counselors are alarmed about the scant amount of time husbands and wives spend with each other during the course of the week, and parents with children. We are a distracted generation. The average family hardly has time to eat a hurried sandwich together, and that is often done in the car after we have zipped through a drive-through where someone hands our food to us through our car window.

I recently heard a couple of marriage counselors suggest than any marriage can be improved by committing to a 30/30 plan—spending thirty minutes together for thirty days. Your calendar can make that happen. A thoughtfully planned schedule is the way to protect priceless moments with those most precious to us. Block in date nights, family times, camping trips, regular meals, getaway weekends, and reading times with your youngsters at bedtime. Use your calendar as a shield to encircle and protect the most important things of life.

I have found that backward goal setting is critical. If I have a project due on, say, December 15, I look at my yearly calendar and, breaking down the project into its logical components, insert the deadlines into my calendar in advance. If it is a book deadline, I need the first chapter finished by March 1. I need the basic draft of the whole book by November 1. By plugging these intermediate steps into my calendar, it helps keep the project moving.

An elaborate science has evolved around this, of course. Just consider how NASA plans a space mission with multiple operations and thousands of components being synchronized to a split second, sometimes years in advance. Corporations, organizations, businesses, and churches use complex computer models and planning grids to work backward from a launch or rollout date, making sure every component is integrated onto a comprehensive planning grid.

Few of us have projects that require labyrinthine complexity. It is just a matter of thinking ahead and giving thought to our "steps." If you want to run the marathon, when do you need to start training? What do you need to do the week before the event? Two weeks before? A month before? Two months before? Insert your training schedule into your calendar. By working in reverse, you know the way forward. This is the meaning of the famous Chinese proverb that says, "The journey of a thousand miles must begin with a single step."

Big projects can be overwhelming, but anyone can take small steps. In my book *The Red Sea Rules* I suggest that when we are unsure what to do, we just need to take the next logical step by faith. If we are paralyzed by procrastination and are facing dilemmas that have no simple solutions, we just have to ask ourselves, "What little step can I take right now toward addressing this?"

It is not that we have to be busy every moment; some of those moments are for closing our eyes, breathing deeply, relaxing our muscles, resting, praying, or meditating. Just do not waste them. Gather the fragments of time and use them. Make the most of odd moments. Take advantage of spare minutes. Do not waste your waits. Do not let the hours flitter away, and do not toss away the moments. When you have invested the hours and tackled the big tasks, gather the fragments that remain, so that nothing is lost.

You can do a lot with life's spare change.

Working with Busy Pastors and Church Staff
Ed Jent

I love to backpack in the Smoky Mountains. Backpacking is about figuring out just how many ounces you can leave behind. I have friends who cut off half of their toothbrush handle to get rid of a few grams. However, I had one friend who went backpacking with me and loaded his pack with some pretty nifty items if you were preparing to compete on the Food Network or to join the U.S. Army's Special Forces for an assault on Baghdad. We had traveled less than three miles and he was exhausted; within five miles his knees were swollen to the size of grapefruit.

Each time we stopped, another friend and I started taking items out of the first friend's pack and placing them in ours, thus making the journey easier for him but tougher on us. We were happy to do it; he is a great guy! However, he is no longer a backpacker. Although he loved the idea of hiking across the mountains and enjoying the beautiful scenery, he decided a good hotel with a bellhop to carry his bags is more his style.

Pastors and church staff all agree that the most valuable resource we have are church members and, although we love all of them, church members fall into one of two groups: those who put things in your pack and those who take things out of the pack. Imagine yourself taking a backpacking trip with a group of people; if you are not a backpacker, envision luggage without wheels instead. Our mission is to complete the journey by lightening one another's loads and there are several things we can do to make the journey easier.

Working with pastors and staff is where experience, passion, and personality meet; mixing these is sure to result in a variety of outcomes. These are the things leaders want in their backpacks along with a few things leaders want to keep out.

Items That Have to Be Included in the Pack

Clarity

Nothing warms my heart like someone who can present an idea well without having to describe those small nuances that, albeit important, are unnecessary to the decision needing to be made. Clarity is sometimes best when the end result is presented first. When someone knows what will be accomplished, the other details make much more sense. An opening statement might look something like this: "Pastor I want to talk to you about (_____). These are the steps I plan to take to accomplish this goal …."

With a good opening statement you grab the attention of your pastor/staff. The more succinctly you can do that, the easier it becomes to elicit a favorable response.

A List of Resources Needed

Completing any project is easier if you have the correct equipment or tools. Request items you will need to complete a task as early as possible. Projects may require you to recruit specific manpower, develop flyers or posters, print and distribute literature, or secure permission from other organizations. A no-surprise approach to a ministry project is always welcome. Understandably, there are items you cannot control, but include a miscellaneous category in your plans.

One of the greatest folks I have ever worked with was a woman who was a creative genius. Anything she planned was always fun and the people involved had a great time. However, every idea was always a few leaves short of being in the shade. Eventually, I learned to plan for these shortfalls, but working with her would have been much easier if she had just thought ahead.

A Budget

The items you need to complete a project almost always require an approved purchase order. The problem is that a middle-of-the-year idea does not have a line item dedicated to the great idea you have birthed. Carefully identify the items you need and how much financing your project requires. A detailed list is very helpful when you have a great idea.

Backpacking has taught me many lessons, but the primary one is that, once you leave on the trail, you better have the items you need; if you do not, there is no convenience store on the trail. Take the time to budget for the items you will need and then stick to your plan. Your efforts will be greatly appreciated if you take the time to present a list that outlines the needed items with a researched cost associated with each.

A Time Line

A time line communicates you have your game plan ready. When we backpack we have to determine when we will arrive at each shelter or campsite. A time line provides built-in checkpoints so that participants communicate to everyone else what is getting done or, in some cases, what is going undone. Accountability is enhanced when we have a time associated with a task. Busy pastors/staff are thankful when they have something they can review that allows them to gauge the progress of a ministry they have authorized. The document does not have to be fancy; a simple explanation of where you want to be, complete with the date you plan to be there, is sufficient.

A List of Obstacles You May Encounter

Are obstacles really obstacles if they are on a pre-planned list? Sure they are, though they are not surprises. When you can predict items that have the potential to slow or derail a project, you can also develop contingency plans for those items. Your professional staff loves to solve problems, but you become a great asset when you can manage items that have already been thought out. Some of these items would include these questions: What do I do if it rains? What do I do if attendance exceeds my room size? What do I do if a speaker is delayed?

Then there are questions that you can check ahead of time: Are thermostats set appropriately? Do I have spare projector bulbs? Do I have honorariums in hand? Have I planned for extra seating? Do I have a checklist of major items to be completed? Have I delegated properly? Have I communicated effectively?

All of these questions will diminish obstacles you are likely to encounter.

Tips for Communicating with Staff

Recognize situations that are not conducive to presenting your plans. This may seem obvious, but the desire to get things done when it is convenient sometimes overwhelms common sense. If you have important work to do for the Lord, do not diminish its importance by trying to get it done after a service or in a hallway conversation.

Write down your plan in an organized fashion and leave a copy with the person. This will eliminate misunderstandings about what is to be accomplished and will provide a reference point for your staff to present your ideas to others for approval. A well-organized document is something that will provide a reference point for your pastor through the approval, preparation, instigation, and completion of your ministry project.

Send progress updates. It is encouraging to get e-mail that describes the exciting work being completed. Photos are also welcomed. A pastor may be busy at certain intervals during the year, but seeing your work in progress is always a blessing.

Learn the personality of the person you are working with. Everyone has strengths and weaknesses. Everyone has specific ways they like to have things presented to them. Take the time to observe the characteristics of the person you are working with and operate accordingly. Remember there is nothing wrong with asking how someone wants something presented: "Is it okay if I e-mail you my plan in advance or would you rather I present to you in person when we meet to discuss it?" Always make an appointment.

Items to Keep Out of the Pack

Inflexibility

Remember your pastor/staff is looking at a big picture while you are often looking at one component. Your idea may be a great one but your timing may be off. Do your best to understand when adjustments are made to your plan. In every organization there are competing priorities; managing those is no small task.

Closed-Mindedness

Open your mind to new suggestions, ideas, and adjustments. Adjusting a few items sometimes creates a better fit. See suggestions and actions of fine-tuning as appreciation for your plan or as a desire on behalf of the person doing the adjusting to be involved in what you have created. Closed-mindedness will limit the participation of others when it should be our desire to involve as many as possible.

Criticism/Sarcasm

Criticism is the weight that unknowingly weighs down a person on his journey. Words we use, and the manner in which we present them, do much to enhance or hinder our journey. Always think about ways you can help carry the load instead of slipping in unnecessary words that hinder the progress of your journey.

> Let us hold fast the profession of our faith without wavering; (for he is faithful that promised;) And let us consider one another to provoke unto love and to good works: Not forsaking the assembling of ourselves together, as the manner of some is; but exhorting one another: and so much the more, as ye see the day approaching. (Heb. 10:23–25)

> Let your speech be always with grace, seasoned with salt, that ye may know how ye ought to answer every man. (Col. 4:6)

Church members are the greatest resource in the church. I know I have no greater joy than to see someone successfully navigate through a ministry to reap from the fields that are white unto harvest.

Strategic Planning
Randal D. Ongie

Every church is uniquely created and gifted by God to affect the lives of people. With that being said, I am amazed that churches often look for their direction in all the wrong places. Some listen to denominational guidelines, others follow past traditions that were effective in their day, still others try to imitate the latest, greatest church that is packing the seats in weekend services and in their own brand of "how to do church" conferences. Do not get me wrong. We can and should learn from all of these sources, but what we learn should never substitute for direction. I would like to challenge you to find a better, more biblical way to lead with strategic direction and clarity. A commitment to prayer and following a process that allows God to give you direction uniquely designed for your church is a great starting point. You probably understand a commitment to prayer, so let us focus on what a strategic planning process might look like.

The Three-Box Planning Model

Every church should plan well and then commit to clear communication about the plan. I believe God has given us (as leaders of His flock) a ministry opportunity that should be maximized for His glory. This is true stewardship. If you will embrace this motivation for planning and communication, you will be effective regardless of the form you follow. I would like to give you some principles in planning to help you act on this motivation.

I recently met with a church board and learned that they had some confusion about how to lead effectively without getting too involved in the details. They felt the weight of leadership but did not know how to live that out appropriately. I began our session by drawing three rectangular boxes on the white board, one under the next in vertical alignment. In the first box, I wrote these words: *mission*, *vision*, *values*, and *DNA*. In the second box, I wrote the word *strategies*. Finally, in the bottom box, I wrote the word *tactics*.

I started our discussion by focusing on the top box. Without exception, a church's top leadership group should always be responsible for this box. Since the effectiveness of your ministry is dependent on aligning all of your effort under these concepts, it is critical that you understand what belongs at this level. Here is a brief glossary of terms:

> **Mission:** Your mission is your purpose, the reason that you exist.
> **Vision:** Your vision is the big idea(s) of how you will accomplish your mission.
> **Values:** Your values are who you are or what makes you a unique church. These are nonnegotiables, key distinctives, your identity as a church.
> **DNA:** Your DNA is all of the above plus some.

If you study the biological role of DNA, you will find it is the code written in each cell that not only can replicate itself, but the whole organism. When applied to the church body, it is a powerful image that each member has the potential to carry the code for the entire church within him or her. As an example, I have seen members of a church—built on a foundation of caring relationships and living life together in small-group settings—live out that code in new settings and situations. Invisible, but very real, this code provides affirmation to leadership and the entire church when the direction of leadership is consistent with it. It is equally real when members react to direction that seems to be at odds with the code. To lead effectively, especially in times of change, this DNA must be understood and addressed.

For you to lead with clarity, it is important that you know and articulate who you are as a unique church, created by God for specific purposes. The less clear you are about whom you are as a church and why you exist, the harder it will be to effectively plan and execute ministry. As I continued the discussion with the aforementioned church board, I discovered that they had some ambiguity about who they were. I encouraged them to spend some time doing a values-clarification exercise and some visioning work prior to moving to the second box.

It is important to consistently communicate "top-box" issues to the church. Life is busy and people can lose sight of the big picture. It is good to be reminded about whom they are collectively and what God has called them to do. I have never worked with a church that was accused of overcommunication.

The second box is where strategic planning occurs. By definition, strategies are large movements or initiatives designed to begin to "live out" your vision. These initiatives should provide guidance and priority for the next two or three years. Most churches and other organizations would be wise to limit their number of major initiatives to four or five. Remember the old adage "too many priorities equal no priority." The biggest temptation I see in most strategic plans is to overdo the number of initiatives, which adds too much complexity. This comes from a desire to accomplish a lot in a short amount of time but often leads to ambiguity, ineffectiveness, and discouragement.

Three-Question Leadership

Every leader would be well served to remember a principle that I learned a few years ago. I call it "Three-Question Leadership." If you will remember that your congregation wants these three questions answered, you will be well on your way to more effective leadership:

1. Is God in this?

2. Have I and the other leaders thought this through?

3. What should I do as a follower?

The first question gives you a chance to cast vision. The second should encourage you to not only plan well but also to communicate well. Once God has given your team a plan for the future, work hard to communicate it with clarity. If the first two questions are handled well, people will be excited to hear about how they can participate.

The Planning Process

Every planning process should follow a basic flow. Plan, act, evaluate, and then plan again. This type of planning rhythm will allow learning and adjustment from year to year, and help the congregation gain clarity and confidence in what God is calling the church to be and to do.

I encourage you to have a designated time every year for planning. Fall is the beginning of the year for most ministries; students are back in school, family vacations are over, and new people have moved and settled in over the summer months. Many churches arrange their fiscal year to coincide with their ministry year. This makes budgeting much easier for staff and key volunteers who will implement the plan.

Your planning team should be made up of top-level leaders, pastors and ministry staff, as well as key lay leaders, if they will be asked to lead a ministry area. I like to start every planning session by doing three things:

1. Perform a reality check for the top box and remind everyone whom we are and why God placed us here.

2. Look at relevant data, both qualitative and quantitative.

3. Review last year's plan and ask what has been done and how has it served us. It is also important to note what went wrong and why, and what was learned along the way. The more honest your assessment is of where you are, the more effective you will be going forward.

Evaluate the top box and everyone's understanding of how to articulate why you exist and what God has called you to do. Occasionally, you will want to do some vision work (not more often than every five to seven years) to renew your commitment to your vision and to modify language used to clearly communicate who you are and why you exist. Revisioning is not part of normal strategic planning but is critical to long-term effectiveness. Churches vary in how they originate vision. Some rely on a single visionary leader or a few visionary leaders, and others use a group process for visioning. Either way, the vision will need to be touched and shaped by several people to be deeply understood and fully implemented. This process will also hone the vision into a clear and compelling concept that will serve to move the church forward as one.

When choosing data to use in planning, be sure that you count the same things every year during the same time frame and the in same way. One of my favorite numbers is average worship attendance because it is very quantifiable. It serves you well, when taken for the same time period every year and counted in the same way as described above. For example, you cannot include special Christmas services one year and not the next. The important thing about quantitative data is it reveals trends over several years. Another way to use worship attendance is as a control number. As an example, if your actual giving for the last year was $600,000 and your average worship attendance was 469 people, then you can calculate your dollars given per worship attendee last year at about $1,279. This can be done with many core numbers such as adults in small groups or adults in Sunday school. If you notice that your worship attendance is growing by 7 percent per year but your percentage of adults in small groups is dropping in relationship to average worship attendance, you will want to find out why and plan appropriate changes. This can be done for every area of ministry. You will find it is quite simple if you make a commitment to collecting solid, quantitative figures.

Qualitative data, on the other hand, can be harder to gather and must be handled with care. However, it is vital for increased ministry effectiveness. Some churches use feedback from new attendees to evaluate their assimilation strategy. Increasing numbers of churches are using church-wide surveys to gather vital qualitative data. Some of the best surveys ask people to rate their walk with God or spiritual growth. Before you do this, it is important to agree on what you must know to lead more effectively, and limit the survey to the most important things. I have seen churches on both extremes, some with no data for planning and evaluation and others drowning in too much data.

After you have reviewed last year's plan and gotten an update on progress, it is time to make a list of issues that needs to be addressed. Out of all of the issues stated, the group should pick the top four or five that are most critical and begin to develop strategies that address them over the next few years. Some of these might have been in your previous plan and just need to be continued. Others might be new approaches to increase effectiveness. The most critical thing is that the board or top leadership group must be sure that these strategies align with your "top box." Alignment is a critical responsibility for this level of leadership.

Once this work is done and drafted into a strategic plan, the staff and key volunteers are free to work on the bottom box that we labeled *tactics*. Tactics should translate into an annual ministry plan for the next ministry year. This plan should be in alignment with the strategic plan and add some specificity to it. For instance, the strategic plan may call for a shift from a Sunday school model in children's ministry to a large group/small group format. This is no small change; the children's pastor will have to think through what needs to happen early on to bring about that change, and what he or she can accomplish in this ministry year. The annual plan should have a series of very specific action items with an owner (person responsible for leading the effort) and a completion date for each item. It might look something like this:

> **Action:** Review three curriculum choices for large group/small group children's ministry format and make recommendations to staff leadership team.
> **By:** December 31, 2010
> **Who:** Pastor Smith

As the annual plan is developed, the pastor and/or staff leadership will need to watch for alignment to the strategic plan and for integration of staff effort. If too many activities are planned for the same time, they can compete for communication, volunteer support, and other resources. These efforts need to be wisely integrated so the church can move forward together. Remember, less is more when it comes to activity. Focus on the things that will get you closer to what God has created you to do.

Planning is a process, not an event. As you commit to good evaluation of whom God has created you to be and where you are going next, you will be able to gain clarity that will aid leaders and followers alike. The increase in ministry effectiveness will be worth the effort.

Planning with Perspective
Kurt Jenkins

It Is All About Perspective

I have never been to the Grand Canyon, but I have heard the experience is completely different depending on whether you tour the site in a helicopter or on a donkey. The view, the weather, the terrain, and even the smells can differ greatly depending on your perspective. One person returning from the Grand Canyon may have loved the trip, praising the beautiful view of God's creation and the comfort of the tour. (I guarantee that he will be a return customer.) Someone else may return with stories of painful mountain climbs on rough terrain coupled with the extreme heat of mid-summer. (I am not so sure this person's perspective will lead to a return visit.) From your perspective you gain insight and opinions about your experiences, responsibilities, and life as a whole.

Organizing church functions has everything to do with your perspective. First and foremost, you need a positive attitude about the administration required to organize with a biblical perspective. Paperwork and planning do not seem like world-changing duties, but God's anointing is provided for those who are called to administration (see Rom. 12:6–8; and 1 Cor. 12:27–28). These gifts are important in God's kingdom since they help organize information so God and His people can get together. That is the kingdom perspective: to effectively plan church functions that create an atmosphere and environment where people can connect with God. Whether through relationships, an encounter with God Himself, or an introspection of one's walk with God, organizing church functions is about God, not the administration.

It is time church leaders stop riding on donkeys and start flying in helicopters. We will then begin seeing the big picture of organizing church functions instead of getting lost in the dust of the details. I hope the following levels of perspective will help you begin organizing highly effective church functions where God shows up and does amazing things.

The Helicopter Level

Helicopter rides are all about the view. The perspective from that height is one of awe and excitement. You see a snapshot of an entire region and landscape, without having to focus in on the details. In ministry planning, this is often called "zooming out." Before the details and decisions get overwhelming, we must zoom out and get a greater perspective.

The first question you need to answer is "What are we trying to accomplish?" Stated differently, "What is the main purpose for having the function in the first place?" If you cannot answer this question, you may have a sacred cow in your church calendar that needs to die. If you can come up with a clear (and biblical) purpose for what you are trying to accomplish, you can begin moving forward with a planning team or committee.

Brainstorming is a great way to get a Helicopter Level perspective on a church function. Effective brainstorming helps keep the purpose of your function the center focus while still allowing a creative flow of ideas to come from your planning team. However, this type of planning is no longer a practice in many churches. In fact, we can probably argue that creative thinking is a lost art in the church. We have somehow left big dreaming to the business and entertainment industries. We serve the God who created the heavens and the earth (Gen. 1:1; Ps. 146:5–6), but we often fail to allow the Spirit of God who lives in us to flow creatively through us. Planning teams need to put their dreaming caps back on and begin looking at church functions from that one, dynamic, creative, biblical perspective—one that anticipates God showing up and doing amazing things through your plans; one that organizes events that are larger than the church can handle with its own manpower and money; one that brings creativity back into the church so we can invent better ways of doing the same old events. This type of aggressive creativity will be sure to spark life into your average church functions.

Here is an example of how you can brainstorm at the Helicopter Level. First, gather a team of people who are passionate, or at least knowledgeable, about the upcoming event. Write the title and main goals of the function in the center of a white board or poster board, and let your team begin to dream of big ideas that would create an event that accomplishes your purpose. Add different categories as ideas come up and simply organize it all around the central theme. Keep the main idea central throughout the discussion, and do not allow finances, resources, volunteers, or any other earthly excuse limit an idea given. Everything goes at this level.

The Skyscraper Level

It will eventually be time to land your helicopter and take in the view from the top of a skyscraper. This perspective still encompasses a broad panoramic landscape, but some details come into focus at this level. For instance, you can see people walking on sidewalks, specific traffic patterns, and numerous activities you would not see from a helicopter. The same holds true while organizing church functions.

There comes a time where some big decisions need solidifying, and this occurs at the Skyscraper Level. The first decision to make is to set the date, time, and location in which to host your event. You may have assumed a certain date or location was best, but that may very well change once you release your team to brainstorm creatively. You cannot allow last year's calendar to determine this year's event. So many times we let a piece of paper tell us how and where to host a function, whether it has been working or not. Think fresh each year for recurring events and make decisions that will best create an environment for people to connect with God.

The Skyscraper Level is also where your planning team must take all of the creative ideas and categorize them into departments. The graphic on page 63 shows some of the categories already in place, but new ones can be created at this point so certain areas have greater attention given to them. Each department will be assigned a department coordinator at this level. Recruiting the right coordinators for each department will have a huge bearing on the effectiveness of the entire event.

Department coordinators should fall under the leadership of the event director, or pastor, who is ultimately responsible for the function. Recruiting strong people at this level helps duplicate your leadership since they will be recruiting volunteers alongside you in their specific area. They also take responsibility for the success of their departments, which develops everyone's delegation skills (see Ex. 18:22–23; Acts 6:1–7). If you do not recruit department coordinators at this level, get ready to do all of the work yourself while organizing this event. Remember, God has gifted others in areas in which you are not as talented in order for His whole body to be in use (see 1 Cor. 12).

The Ground-Floor Level

Once you have your date, location, and coordinators in place, you can jump on the elevator and go to the ground floor. This perspective brings with it everything you would picture happening on the ground floor of a skyscraper. The mail is being sorted, bills are being paid, the trash is being collected, and the boiler room is operating full force. These activities usually go unnoticed by the average person, but they are vital to the success of every corporate building.

For every church function you organize, there is a Ground Floor perspective just waiting to be visited. There are countless tasks that go into every successful event that no one will ever notice. But the work needs doing, and should be done as if we are working unto the Lord (see Eph. 6:5–7). At this perspective, all of your brainstorming ideas get tested for practicality. Some things will go smoothly, but many require several attempts before moving forward. Proverbs 12:24 says, "The hand of the diligent shall bear rule: but the slothful shall be under tribute." Your coordinators will be faced with the challenge of recruiting diligent volunteers for the specific tasks they will identify at this level. If God has supplied the funds and resources by this stage of the planning, then each department should decide on the specific activities that will be included in the event. On the following page is a sample planning template you can use to organize your functions.

You should be asking questions such as:

1. "What specifically needs to be accomplished for _____ to be in place for the function?"

2. "How many and what kind of volunteers are needed for each activity within the departments?"

3. "What are the specific materials I will need to supply the volunteers so their job can be done effectively?"

4. "How much is budgeted for each department?"

The more questions you can answer now, the better organized your function will be. The Ground Floor is often the most frustrating stage of planning, but it can also be the most enjoyable and rewarding.

ANNUAL CHURCH PICNIC
Sunday, July 11th – Community Park and Playground

Purpose & Goals
1. To provide an opportunity for church attendees to fellowship and build new friendships
2. To connect with community residents through outreach activities during the picnic
3. To promote VBS, fall small groups and ongoing ministries of our church to all visitors

Overview

Our annual church picnic will be held this year at the Community Park and Playground. We chose to host this event at a public location to attract more community residents as a form of outreach. We will also provide the entire event for free. In addition to a full scale cookout, there will be games, activities, helpful resources and ministry stations available. All are invited to attend this event with a friend, relative or neighbor.

When & Where
- Sunday, July 11th
- 11am – 3pm (Includes two 2-hour volunteer shifts)
- Community Park and Playground

Departments and Volunteer Teams

| FOOD DEPT. | | MINISTRY & HELPS DEPT. | | ENTERTAINMENT | | |
| Coordinator: | | Coordinator: | | Coordinator: | | |
Grilling	Desserts	Financial Advice	Prayer Team	Carnival Games	Dunk Tank	Misc.
First Shift (11am – 1pm)						
1	1	1	1	1	1	1
2	2	2	2	2	2	2
Second Shift (1pm – 3pm)						
1	1	1	1	1	1	1
2	2	2	2	2	2	2
Notes						

Sample Materials	Qty.	Estimated Cost	
Giveaway Bibles			
Grill and grilling equipment			
Hot dogs, hot dog buns, ketchup			
Cases of soda, bottled water			
Promotion			
Invitation cards			
Outdoor banner			
Bulletin insert			

Perspectives in Review

Organizing church functions takes a team of people planning from different perspectives. Whether you are soaring in a helicopter, looking down from a skyscraper, or pounding the pavement from the ground floor, these functions are still about connecting people with God. It is not the fancy decor, not the celebrity speaker, not the number of donations that matter, but people and God.

Setting Policies
Stephen Helm

Policies are pathways. Whether you are in a large or small church you already have policies. They may be written or unwritten, but they do exist.

I first experienced this in my first church of thirty people. I was twenty-one years of age, the "new guy." I started a youth group that would fit in my car. Christmas holidays were coming, so I thought it would be a great thing to have my "group" make cookies and deliver them to shut-ins in our community. Since the motivation behind this project was pure, since it would help people, and since it would take no church money, in my mind it was a slam dunk idea, not requiring a business meeting or any permission.

The part of the scenario I did not anticipate was that, evidently, the church kitchen was sacred—more sacred than any other place in the building. Items carefully and perfectly stacked in the cupboards were not there to be used, necessarily. I had no idea, and apparently sinned boldly.

After cleaning the kitchen to what we thought was "the same as we found it" standard, I got a call late that evening. The voice on the other end of the phone was very disturbed that "someone" had broken into the church, used the kitchen, and left it a wreck. I reluctantly came clean and took my verbal woodshed "education." I had violated an unwritten policy.

Depending on the size or culture of your church, "rules and regulations" defining how things get done may or may not be all neatly included in a bound document. Some are passed along through oral tradition. However, the greater the number of people leading, creating, and serving, the greater the need becomes to pass this along more formally.

Biblical Examples

The apostle Paul, traveling from place to place, found it necessary to do more than talk about how the infant church was to rock the crib. He constantly communicated defined pathways (policies) to reinforce or create order and process. Here are just a few examples from 1 Corinthians:

1. Divisions in the church (1 Cor. 3)

2. Apostleship/Leadership (1 Cor. 4, 9)

3. Dealing with an immoral brother (1 Cor. 5)

4. Legal challenges among Christ followers (1 Cor. 6)

5. Church organization (1 Cor. 12:12–14:39)

6. Honoraria and giving (1 Cor. 16)

Keep Policies in Check

A "good" policy has a destination, or defined result. A policy needs to be rethought or challenged if the only reinforcement as to why it is still a policy is "we've always done it that way."

It is important to remember that policies are not the purpose of your church. Neither do they make good replacements when the purpose or vision may be unclear. Policies serve by helping to streamline practical ways to accomplish tasks effectively. The result of all policies should be to help achieve the "cause" or mission of your organization. Policies that do not directly advance your mission cost your church time, energy, and other resources, ultimately impeding forward motion.

The purpose of your church may stay the same for a very long time. You may articulate and restate your purpose over time to freshen it up, but best practices and policies require constant feedback and honest review. This will ensure that time and energy are invested in moving the mission forward rather than repeating practices that are less effective, taking the organization sideways or backward.

A colleague of mine in a large church would frequently say, "Organizations produce what they are designed to produce." Sounds simple enough, but many choose tactics and procedures before determining their destination and wonder why they never arrive where they want. A simple example: Starbucks makes really good coffee but would be lousy at changing the oil in my car. Why? Starbucks has designed their stores, equipment, processes, and trained their staff for one goal: coffee experience, not auto repair. If after all that work, narrowing what they do well, a store manager had the great idea of now adding an oil change option to the drive through, the experience would totally miss the mark, leaving people scratching their heads.

Our policies follow the articulation of direction and work together like parts of a machine to get us to where we are called to go. Simply doing more of the same things that do not produce what we want will only produce more of what we do not want. Again, that is a simple thought, but follows the classic definition of insanity.

On the subject of insanity, it is important to consider that a good set of policies will not cover every exception or every contingency. When exceptions emerge—and they will—it is more helpful to rely on the chain of command/responsibility (i.e., a pastor/supervisor, team leader, administrative board or team). Failing to keep policies few and simple can amass documentation requiring one to have a law degree, which no one will read or use, and again gets in the way of advancing your mission.

There are, however, people wired to be extremely excited over formulating policies. They can be very helpful if their advice is taken in small doses. If they are given the reins on policy making, however, you may as well rename your church "Rules Are Us."

When is a new policy needed? When it seems that the same issue keeps emerging, it reveals a lack of a clear pathway. When members make up their own route to accomplish something, it is not a sign of bad behavior. It is more often a signal that a clearly defined pathway can help good people accomplish goals more effectively.

You should check the following types of policies:

1. Operational Policies

   Operational policies are typically financial or personnel related. They define pathways that are accountable and measurable. These are the easiest to create and review. When they are ineffective, vague information or even chaos is the result, indicating the need for change. As invisible as operational policies may seem, many churches have suffered considerable damage when these policies were either weak or unenforced. For instance, many churches have a policy that their pastors are not money handlers, nor do they have direct access to church finances. Is it that pastors are not to be trusted with the finances? Not at all. Having this in place guards both the congregation and the pastors if financial handling is ever questioned. Another example might be having job descriptions for every employee. This establishes a basis for future conversation regarding a person's job effectiveness and accounts for instances when a person far exceeds expectations and there needs to be a reconsideration of the person's compensation.

2. Risk Management

   Risk Management policies are pathways that guard either the people or the organization, or both, such as within children's ministry, youth ministry, adult ministry, professional/ pastoral relationships, buildings, and grounds. Examples include adult-to-child ratios in classrooms; procedures for taking children to restrooms; transportation for youth to events, campus, and so on; who can drive, and what vehicles can be used; when you require release forms; security measures required when transporting offerings from the church building to a bank; liability issues involving building and grounds used by outside organizations or members; incident reporting, such as for on-site medical treatments or accidents; and staff-related issues (paid leave, performance reviews, and so on).

3. Continued Improvement

Whereas the previous two points are more administrative in nature, continued improvement policies involve defining the pathways toward objectives. These are typically time specific with stated results. One example might be a challenge to all the classes or small groups in a church to change their pattern of meeting during a spiritual emphasis campaign to include new members, study the same curriculum, or elect a project to be completed by a certain date with pictures and stories to share with the whole church.

Another example of this policy might be found in designating the use of the church facility during a disaster (hurricane, flood, etc.). If there are no short-term policies for continued improvement, it might mean too little experimentation is being done to discover new ways of doing ministry.

Embrace Collaborative Review

Ultimately, there has to be a place and a specific group of people who are responsible for reviewing policies, their effectiveness, their fit with culture, and their goals. If left to smaller circles of people who are never sitting down together to talk these out, the policies will not take all factors into account. They might serve small purposes, but collide with the greater purposes.

Ideally, policies are not created in a vacuum. Rather, where possible, collaboration can generate shared ownership and reinforce their effectiveness. The inverse is also true: if radical change is dictated with little or no lead time and no collaborative discussion preceding the change, resistance is almost always the result.

Pushback is not sin. It is not disloyalty; neither is it disagreement with a good or necessary idea toward change. When opposition emerges it simply indicates the "change rate" your leadership culture can handle has been exceeded. Here is a simple equation I have found true and learned by the pain of ignoring:

[Speed of change] − [information] = [overspending your leadership chips].

Changing too quickly is a rookie mistake, but many have managed to make a painful and disappointing career of it. If you want to be a church leader who fosters an atmosphere of mistrust, changing too quickly will do it better than anything else.

How to Create Workable Policies

1. State an objective consistent with the "dream" or vision of your church.

2. Define who is affected by that objective (i.e., new attendees, groups of people, those interested in a specific affinity).

3. Define the pathway and practice that needs to be created or challenged.

4. State the desired outcome (i.e., quantity, time frame), remembering, "If you can measure it, you can manage it."

5. Name when and who will review the outcomes.

Policies are to your church what bones are to your body: if they show, there is probably something very wrong. The church staff, leaders, and key volunteers will know your policies. Some might even be posted on the church Web site if intended for all to follow (i.e., wedding policies). What should show outwardly, however, is the warmth of genuine welcome and hope that life can be different, made possible not by our policies, but through Christ.

Part Three
Relationships

Unity and Diversity
Dr. Doug Dees

I realize the chapter title is "Unity and Diversity." But I think it is best that we think about it as "Unity within Diversity." We are really shooting at both at the same time. We can have both. We should want both. I think that in looking at it this way, we will create less of a linear compartmentalized church structure.

Our Lord wants us to be unified in who we are as a people. After all, He, His Father, and the Holy Spirit are One. And He desires that of us:

> And all mine are thine, and thine are mine; and I am glorified in them.And now I am no more in the world, but these are in the world, and I come to thee. Holy Father, keep through thine own name those whom thou hast given me, that they may be one, as we are. (John 17:10-11)

He also wants us to reach all nations as He asks in the Great Commission. When we take our eyes off of Christ and His mission, we will focus on something else. Only He can bring unity to a body of believers. When we take our eyes off of Christ, we also lose our diversity. We begin looking at our differences instead of our similarities in Him. Paul says, "I am made all things to all men, that I might by all means save some" (1 Cor. 9:22b). Are we willing to do that? Or do we have ideas of what we want church to be and thus pursue those things?

It is possible to be unified and diverse at the same time. It is possible to have many ministries all carrying out the same focus in differing ways. The greatest challenge is to create consensus that there is one main purpose and then to execute diverse methods of carrying out this purpose through various means. It is possible, but certainly not easy. Proverbs 19:21 reminds us, "There are many devices in a man's heart; nevertheless the counsel of the LORD, that shall stand."

Taking a lot of ideas of what is important and boiling them down to one main purpose can take time. And trying to evaluate whose purpose you are working toward, God's or man's, is tough. But I believe it is worth it. Once you get there, everyone will feel they have been part of the process and part of the success. Many ministries can follow the same purpose but carry it out differently: unity within diversity, and diversity within unity.

Purpose/Vision/Ministry

It works best in this order: Purpose/Vision/Ministry. Ask this question: What did God promise your city when He created your church? I hope He was the driving force behind your church coming into existence. What is His ongoing desire for your local body of believers? How are you carrying it out? By diversifying your efforts, how can you do what you do in His Kingdom where you are?

First and foremost, of course, our purpose needs to be the same one: His!

Jesus said the greatest commandment is to love God and to love others (Matt. 22:36-40). Can that be a unifying purpose people carry out in different ways? Remember how Christ carries out that commandment: He was constantly loving people. He healed them. He taught them. He comforted them. He explained life to them. He explained the kingdom of heaven to them. He fed them. He listened to them. He saved them from stoning. He rebuked them. He showed them tough love. He was and is the master at having a simple purpose but being able to apply it in diverse ways.

There can be many vision statements underneath that overarching purpose statement. But if Jesus saw it as that important, then I need to also.

The vision statement you may have, which helps you define some of the *hows* of the purpose statement, is crucial. If it is not His vision for your church, then you will miss the target. You have to ask God, "What do you see us being here for? How do you want us to carry it out? Show us your way." If you do not tune into what God sees, then what you see may be your own concoction of ideas or a mirrored image of other churches you want to be like. Beware of comparing your church with other churches and mimicking them. Feel free to get ideas from other servants of God; just beware of spiritual plagiarism. God can write a new story at this time in your place. You must get in on His story for Him to write history.

Your ministry statement will then be those actions you plan that carry out the vision God has shown you, which carries out the purpose He has given.

Causes of Disunity

While attempting to move toward unified diversity, you already know there are roadblocks. Satan will attempt to stop you at every turn. I did not say this would be easy. Neither did Christ.

In purposed diversity, you can reach more people for Christ and put more people to work in the kingdom.

The issue here is actually control. If there is a main group of leaders who must know everything and approve everything that happens, then you will limit the amount of diversity and create a logjam of decisions. I am not saying that there should not be groups of leaders who oversee church matters; my main concern here is that they oversee too much to the point of lording it over a group. Leaders who must know every detail of a plan prove they do not trust the people carrying out that plan. The converse is leaders who have no care or control about a plan and allow people to do whatever they want. Much of the time the purpose/vision/ministry plan does not get accomplished and other things do. Sometimes those things are not even what God wants done.

Example: Sunday school or small-group ministry. Do we want attendance or changed lives? You can have both. Changed lives will cause attendance. If the believers in your church can be taught to really understand what it means to disciple as you go, group training and discipling become a celebration of the last week's victories as well as a springboard into the next week of their lives. On the other hand, if groups exist where changed lives are not the purpose, disunity will thrive there.

You may be thinking, "What if we have unity and nothing is changing?" My answer may hurt: you may be unified around an idea that is dead. Or you may be unified around a great idea, but are trying to do it in a way that is dead. Just because a group is unified does not mean there will be great results. If you were on a road trip, on a newly surfaced interstate, making good time, you would be excited about getting to your destination. But if you wanted to go east but were going west, it would be quite a while before you arrive. If you continued on this path, you'd have an ocean or two to cross. Intent and direction are crucial to unity, but the purpose must be God's, not yours. Having consulted with a wide range of churches, I have found this to be the more frequent problem.

Causes of "Dis-Diversity"

When our work for God is defined narrowly and by a few, less seems to be accomplished. When it is defined broadly and administered by many, much more is accomplished for the kingdom.

Take Acts 2 where Peter preached and 3,000 were saved. Then a few days later he preached again and 5,000 men were saved, not including women and children

(Acts 4:4). All the converts went about simply making disciples, precisely what Christ had asked them to do in His last sixty words in Matthew.

Fight Disunity and "Dis-Diversity"

At the church where I serve now, we are currently rethinking how we can follow a streamlined intent, but with broad applications: unity in thought, diversity in action. One of the first tasks is to define exactly what it was Christ has asked us to do: to disciple!

In my book *ReSymbol*, I discuss how we, as those who lead, are to release people, not contain them. Much of our problems in organized religion can be summed up by these two: we attempt to overcontrol that which should be released or set free to do ministry, or we release people to do ministry although they have no central unified focus.

Christ gives us both the freedom to go and the focus when we do. So within His desires for us are both unity and diversity.

The Purpose and Planning of Leadership Retreats

Dr. Earl B. Mason

Spiritual leaders have one of the greatest and most significant privileges of a lifetime: to actively participate in the transformation of others through the work of leading ministry. The primary purpose of church leadership is to fulfill Acts 1:1, in order that the world would know the gospel of Jesus Christ as Lord. Successful achievement is obtained solely through the guidance of the Holy Spirit partnered with effective ministry work. The church is designed to spread the gospel, evangelize the lost, proclaim the good news of Christ, glorify God, and edify fellow believers; this is accomplished through the people whom God sends to that church. Individuals possessing various experiences, gifts, skills, callings, and creativity must be developed to maturity as disciples of Jesus Christ in order to be effective leaders. This process of development requires a continual and reinforcing plan of preaching and teaching God's Word.

Leadership, at its best, is proficient only through a God-inspired vision. It is through vision that leaders are provided the direction and purpose of the local assembly. Vision defines and clarifies the divinely inspired specified purpose for a particular congregation infusing energy, enthusiasm, and excitement to the work of the church. The church I pastor defines vision as "a divinely inspired portrait of possibility, fueled by God's power, accomplished through God's people, for God's purpose, to God's praise." As such, all leaders must embrace as well as understand the significance of vision. Consequently, leadership development becomes the mechanism by which leaders are able to remain persistent, confident, and focused toward the divinely inspired common purpose.

The expectations, responsibilities, and roles of leadership must be defined with clarity in order to accomplish the goals of the church. Hence, those in leadership roles, namely the leadership council at my own church, are expected to accomplish four things based upon Matthew 28:18–20: (1) to evangelize (making disciples); (2) to exalt (proclaiming glad tidings); (3) to edify (promoting spiritual growth through the message of good news); and (4) to exhort (advising and urging forward movement through the Word of God).

Leadership retreats are one tool for ensuring that leaders are engaged and continually attached to the vision of the church. According to *Merriam-Webster's 11th Collegiate Dictionary*, "retreat" means to "withdraw," "remove," or "recede"; thus for your leadership retreat to have maximum impact you must minimize the distractions and capitalize on this time of deliberate withdrawal. Strategically plan your retreat to create an environment that develops and strengthens church leaders while empowering them to fulfill the vision of the church.

Purpose of Leadership Retreats

Retreats provide an opportunity to be still and fully experience the presence of God in unity as leaders. Pray, plan, and implement ministry goals solely based upon the God-given vision of the church. Retreats should be highly interactive and designed to accomplish five things:

1. Encountering God: Deliberately come together to meet with God and others who share the vision of the church and who seek to grow together toward that common end.

2. Separating from outside distractions: Strategically withdraw for the purpose of collective reflection, meditation, dialogue, planning, and action.

3. Renewing energy: Intentionally replenish energy, commitment, and enthusiasm for the fulfillment of the vision.

4. Deepening our commitment: Knowingly open our spirits for exposure to the Holy Spirit's guiding of our thoughts, behaviors, and actions to accomplish the plans of God.

5. Praying: Consciously come together as a community of believers to share experiences, focus our attention, and talk to the Lord about His plans and our work.

Praying for and Planning the Retreat

When planning the retreat, it is important to consider the people who will attend. The retreat must connect each person both to the vision and to one another through content and activities. The content and outcomes of the retreat are developed during pre-retreat planning, prayer, and waiting for God's direction. Such decisions should not be made in haste, as the outcomes must be for the purpose of fulfilling God's plan and God's plan only.

Through prayer, it will become clear how to proceed with the planning of the retreat. There are several categories of questions to consider during this planning phase:

Content and Scheduling Questions

1. What is the focus of the retreat?

2. Who will present or speak at the retreat?

3. How will the content support or enhance the work toward vision fulfillment?

4. What materials will be necessary to support the retreat content?

5. How early or late should you schedule the retreat program?

6. How much "free time" should you incorporate in the schedule?

7. How many days should you spend on the retreat?

8. What evaluation tool will you utilize to assess the retreat effectiveness?

Timing Questions

1. Is this the appropriate time in the church calendar to retreat?

2. What else in the church's activities are tied to the retreat schedule? (E.g., planning for the future, recasting vision, redirecting ministry programs, etc.)

3. Is there a consistent time of the year to retreat?

4. Does this time detract from other essential church activities?

Location/Facility Questions

1. How far away is the retreat location?

2. Is it within a reasonable travel time given the length of the retreat stay?

3. Are there transportation considerations before and during the retreat?

4. Is the location and facility conducive to the content, work, and activities of the retreat? Try to strike the delicate balance between the activities of the retreat site and the goals of the retreat. Site activities could distract from the goals of the retreat.

5. Does the facility environment evoke a sense of withdrawal and thoughtful exchange?

6. What specific individual arrangements and accommodations does the facility offer to meet your group needs? How will rooming assignments be made?

7. How much flexibility does the retreat facility have in its contract in order to address the needs of the group?

8. Are the facility costs commensurate with the church budget? Or are they priced reasonably if participants are to pay? Will participants pay for the retreat on their own? If so, what is the process and the plan? Are there hidden costs that you must consider prior to signing facility contracts?

9. What other costs will need to be considered for the retreat?

Group Management Questions

1. Do you have all the information to communicate to the group?

2. What is the registration process?

3. Do you have all the essential personnel (onsite and church) to manage the retreat details during the retreat?

4. Have you anticipated the needs of the group to ensure success?

Although this list is not exhaustive, it will provide you with a framework of the detailed attention necessary for planning a successful retreat. It is important to remember that this is God's retreat; therefore, remain connected to the Lord's leading when planning.

It Is a Matter of Vision

The subject of vision can be as dry as Ezekiel's bones, and yet it continues to be the underpinning of any successful operation or ministry. Therefore you must infuse some interesting and fun activities into your ministry so that implementation of the vision does not appear dull or dry—emphasizing the fact that entertainment is never the goal but rather a fulfilling, exhilarating experience that will change people's lives. "Where there is no vision, the people perish (Prov. 29:18). The permanence, priority, and the promise of vision must be clearly articulated and understood by all in leadership roles, regardless of level, in the church.

Understanding the importance of vision is essential to productive participation in all ministry work. Also as we see in Proverbs 29:18, if people cannot see what God is doing, they stumble all over themselves; but when they attend to what God reveals, they are most blessed. What the church looks like and how it will perform in the future greatly depend upon how you and I allow God to use us. As such, a comprehensive leadership development plan for spiritual leaders is essential to the powerful mechanism for reinforcing, maintaining, and sustaining the vision, purpose, and plan of God for the church. This plan must be multidimensional to include ongoing and effective communication, leaders' training, and the timing of periodic retreats.

The fluid nature of church membership requires a concerted effort toward continual work that develops our spiritual leaders. The execution of vision is attractive to those with an expansion/pioneering spirit. God has called us to make trails, pave places, and build bridges for others to cross by our work of faith. The expansion/pioneering spirit requires perseverance, patience, and power. Though the vision tarries, we must be willing to wait for it; it will certainly come—not in our own strength, but through the strength of the One who promised.

Recruiting Volunteers
Kevin R. Scruggs

Two are better than one; because they have a good
reward for their labour.
—Ecclesiastes 4:9

Volunteers: we all need them in ministry. I have often
said to myself that if I just had more people we could
do so much more. There are usually two kinds of volunteers. The first type is drafted into service more because
she or he has a pulse than because she or he would be a
good fit for the ministry. I wonder if you have ever had
this happen to you: "We need help this Sunday. You're
breathing. Perfect! You're hired." The volunteer has no
idea what she's being asked to do but she knows there is a
crisis and that she can forego one worship service to help
out. It is a rare thing to have a volunteer walk away from
that with a positive experience. More often than not, the
volunteer feels guilty or frustrated and leaves as quickly
as possible, telling her friends of her experience to serve
as a warning for all.

The second type is the everywhere volunteer. Have
you ever noticed that the same ten people seem to do the
majority of the work while many other people seem content just to watch them? These volunteers are more than
willing to help and are usually at the church more than
you are. While their efforts are admirable, the general
outcome is burnout, usually out of the blue, probably

when you were counting on their help the most. So how do you get the right volunteer? To be honest there is no five-step program to guarantee success, but there are a few things that you can do to increase your odds.

Create a Job Description

Proverbs tells us that where there is no vision, the people perish. Okay, I can hear some of you thinking "Perishing? I'm just looking for some volunteers, not world peace!" Do not worry, your volunteers will not die, at least not physically. If you do not have some type of vision for what you want them to do, they may die of frustration. Before you even consider putting something in the bulletin inviting people to an informational meeting, you need to create a job description. I will admit that this is not an easy process, but it is extremely necessary. This is where you will decide what type of volunteer you want—one who is a good fit, or simply a warm body who will cost you more time and effort down the road.

To prepare a job description, there are a couple of key questions that you need to answer, but before you do anything, spend some time in prayer. Ask God to prepare the person and you as He brings you together.

The first key question you need to ask is "Are there any church requirements for this position?" For example, if this is a teaching position, does the church require that the volunteer be a member? If you do not know, ask someone else in leadership. There is nothing more frustrating than finding a good fit only to discover that you were unaware of some church requirements that either slow down the process or end it altogether. Does there need to be a background check? Check your church's insurance policy. If the position is dealing with children I strongly recommend doing a background check.

The next question you need to answer is "What are the expectations of this position?" In other words, "What is it that I actually want this volunteer to do?" When it comes to volunteering, no one likes surprises. If the position requires the volunteer to be there for monthly staff meetings, or that once a month he needs to stay after church to help clean up, then tell him. If you are looking for a certain set of skills, include it in the description. You will not be able to cover everything, but the more descriptive you can be, the better. Now before we go too far, do not make your list a mile long or you will scare your potential volunteer off before you ever speak to him. Remember, you are asking for a volunteer. Be honest and thorough, but be succinct.

The next question you need to ask is "What's the level of commitment?" In my current ministry, I have some positions that require one's participation every week and I have others activities that occur once a month. Remember, no one likes surprises.

The final question I need to ask is this: "Am I being realistic with this volunteer position?" When you have everything written down, go back and read the details again. Would you volunteer for this position? Ask a trusted friend to read it; get some feedback. You are asking for someone to volunteer time to help you, to work with you, to be on your team. Congratulations, you made it! Your hard work is about to pay off. You are ready to start recruiting.

Start Recruiting

Recruiting can be a very fun task. This is your opportunity to show others your passion for the ministry God has called you to lead. How you present it to others is very important. People want to rally around a cause, not be pressured into doing something out of your desperation. As a leader, you are asking people to be passionate about this opportunity. You cannot expect others to be something you are unwilling to be. Whether they learn of your ministry through a bulletin, a newsletter, or a verbal announcement during a church service, they need to feel your excitement.

Now you wait. If initially no one responds, do not worry. Just be patient. We serve a very big God who knows exactly the person you need.

Interview the Volunteer

"Okay, so I have gone through this process and now I have a few people who seem interested. Now what?" Interview them. If there is one thing I have learned in ministry it is this: it is very difficult and makes you feel uncomfortable to fire a volunteer. You will be working with this person on a regular basis; make sure it is a good fit. If you do not have an application or questionnaire, create one. Do not worry; you have already done most of the heavy lifting already so it should not be too difficult. Plus, once you create this document you can continue to use it as you recruit more volunteers.

Interviewing a potential volunteer is a helpful way to get a feel for the person, and you will be able to watch his body language as you converse. If possible, meet him for lunch or coffee. (You should pay.) This sets the tone that you care about the people who work with you and, even if the volunteer opportunity does not work out, you have an opportunity to connect with someone from your church. Some key topics you will want to cover in the interview would be his relationship with the Lord (get beyond salvation, have him describe it), how long he has been a part of your congregation, whether he agrees with your church's doctrinal statement (even if he is a member, you will still want to ask this question), and so on.

Beyond these questions, there are a few key elements that I would encourage you to cover. If he is married, ask about his marriage: "How does your spouse feel about this?" "How is your marriage?" That may seem intrusive, but you want to communicate that you care about him as a person and you want to get a feel for what is going on at home. Sometimes people will run from their problems and into ministry as a way of escape. You may be opening up Pandora's Box, so it is better to ask up front.

The final key point I would suggest asking is "Why do you think God wants you to serve in this ministry?" You want to know if this is the volunteer's true passion. If you discover he is doing it out of guilt or because his kids are in the ministry, and he does not feel passionate about it, you will be spending time trying to motivate him. If you think he has potential and is willing to take the risk, at least you will be entering the relationship with your eyes wide open.

Initiate a Trial Period

Once the interview process is complete and the volunteer has begun in your ministry, I would suggest you have a trial period. When a new volunteer arrives in your ministry, establish an initial time frame for her and explain why you are doing it. This gives her a way out if she gets into the ministry and it is not what she wanted or thought it was going to be. This also gives you an out if she comes in and starts wreaking havoc in your ministry. You do not want to lose the volunteers you already have. In about a month I would get together with the new recruit and ask her what she thinks. Whether it is positive or negative, you will have the opportunity to receive and give feedback.

Working with volunteers can be one of the most rewarding parts of ministry. Some of my closest friends have been those with whom I have served. The work that you do on the front end will directly impact the amount of work you will have to do on the back end. Take your time, pray a lot, seek out the advice from your current team, and recruit. God has given us all a passion to serve Him doing the things we love to do. Do not worry; volunteers are out there, just waiting for you to ask them to help.

Identifying and Implementing Spiritual Gifts
Lisa Baker

"Say yes to your big yes and no to the rest." That is the motto within my own congregation when it comes to choosing ministries.

"And when Peter saw it, he answered unto the people" (Acts 3:12).

Peter knew he was created to preach. Most people cannot articulate what they were created to do. If they give an answer at all, most default to a talent, a role they have had in ministry, or a skill they have acquired in business. Talents, roles, skills, and jobs are what people can do. Often church leaders accept what a person can do because Western culture defines its people by what they do. Rather than asking, "What can a believer do?" ask, "What does God do through the believer?" This question is only adequately answered by looking at the individual's spiritual gifts.

The New Testament speaks directly to the topic of spiritual gifts, their origin, and their working function in several passages: Romans 12:4–8; 1 Corinthians 12; Ephesians 4:11–16; 1 Timothy 4:14; and 1 Peter 4:10–11.

A good definition of a spiritual gift is a special attribute given by God's Spirit to every member of the body, according to God's grace, for use within the context of the body for the building up of the body. In short, a spiritual gift is the way God manifests Himself through a believer.

Spiritual gift assessments have been designed to guide believers in spiritual gift identification. These indicators may help individuals engage in a self-discovery process that is an important part of finding effective and fulfilling ministries while helping the individuals gain a better understanding of Christ:

> And he gave some, apostles; and some, prophets; and some, evangelists; and some, pastors and teachers; For the perfecting of the saints, for the work of the ministry, for the edifying of the body of Christ. (Eph. 4:11-12)

As believers understand their own personal giftedness (and, equally important, how they are not gifted), they can better know God. Western culture promotes a corporate organizational approach with rewards that are primarily performance based. But God promotes a living organism—a body, working together—and rewards that stem from faith and motives.

Spiritual Gifts Assessments

Perceiving one's spiritual gifts through an assessment process may point out possible ways that believers can best express faith in God the Creator and build up the church through acts of service or ministry. Going back and forth from the assessment results to the question "What ministries appeal to you?" helps individuals sense how God is leading them.

Having a written questionnaire as part of the assessment process can be helpful; it is important to give the participant as many working parts as possible. Such assessments are especially helpful when the questionnaire includes a subjective component that gives believers the challenge to go deeper inside and answer questions concerning personal passions and life experiences. By looking at several components, the believer can find revealing threads.

The world says, "Choose your life. You can be anything you want to be." But God's Word says, "Before I formed thee in the belly I knew thee; and before thou camest forth out of the womb I sanctified thee, and I ordained thee a prophet unto the nations" (Jer. 1:5). Most if not all believers relate to God creating everything, especially human beings, for a holy purpose: to glorify God. Spiritual gifts spotlight what the holy plan looks like for an individual. The gifts do not so much tell where a person will be involved in ministry as how God will show up through the individual or what the ministry will look like.

In trying to discern what one's spiritual gifts might be, ask the question "What are you doing in ministry when things bigger than yourself happen?" Recognize that the something bigger is God. He works through believers to accomplish much bigger things than they could have accomplished on their own. This is what believers want, what churches want: for God to do great things.

By taking spiritual gift assessments, Christ followers simply discover how they perceive themselves as gifted by God. It is an excellent beginning point in ministry. When believers are involved in ministries that are not suited for their giftedness, they tend to rock the boat. Rocking the boat is not moving rhythmically. Christ followers expressing faith from within do not have to work at conforming to a ministry because God is already working through them.

A common misconception is calling assessments tests, which implies passing or failing. No one fails, because no believer is without a gift (see 1 Cor. 12). No one fails because no believer receives a gift ranked lower than another. No one fails because believers do not receive gifts according to spiritual maturity.

Avoid "Ranking" Gifts

No gift is more important than another. We humanize the gifts elevating one over the other, but in God's reality all of the body parts are necessary and equally important. If a seeker cannot find a parking place, the seeker will not hear the Word of God preached. The person with the gift of service who provides help to the seeker makes it possible for the Word to be heard.

Do Not Confuse Spiritual Gifts with Spiritual Maturity

Spiritual maturity is better linked with the fruit of the spirit. Like a piece of fruit, the fruit of the spirit grows when nurtured and tended. Every believer is promised love, joy, peace, patience, kindness, goodness, faithfulness, gentleness, and self-control. These are the nine characteristics that grow from a life relinquished to God's Spirit. Every follower of Christ can expect this transformation as a result of becoming more and more Christlike. Spiritual gifts, however, are God's gifts to give as He pleases for us to receive.

Studies break down spiritual gifts into types and there is debate over whether some of the so-called gifts are gifts at all. On the practical side, rather than debate what is actually a gift, it is far more helpful to assist Christ followers in finding effective ministries in which to serve. That is why written assessments alone are not sufficient and interactive leadership and discipleship are imperative parts of this process.

Review Assessment Results

Talk through the assessment results with the participant. Look at the top few gifts and look at them in relation to the participant's personality, abilities, passions, and experiences. This gives the participant a broader view and discourages the individual from a narrow one-word label. In looking at the top few gifts, the participant can see a preference toward supporting gifts or equipping gifts. Supporting gifts are action oriented. They undergird ministers and ministries. Supporting gifts may be relational in nature like hospitality or mercy, or they may be task oriented like administration or giving.

Equipping gifts are more verbal in nature and ultimately serve the purpose of preparing people for ministry. Equippers may build up believers inside the church with gifts like wisdom, knowledge, and exhortation/encouragement that primarily build up believers, or they may engage culture through gifts like prophecy or evangelism. These are not hard lines that put gifts only inside or outside the church's walls.

Do Not Limit the Possibilities

It is important to recognize that the Spirit uses all kinds of gifts and abilities to build His kingdom. Understanding this helps prevent us as leaders from being overly stringent in how we place members into ministry, which is the ultimate goal of the assessment process. For example, note what the Lord says about the building of the tabernacle in Exodus 31:1-6:

> And the LORD spake unto Moses, saying, See, I have called by name Bezaleel the son of Uri, the son of Hur, of the tribe of Judah: and I have filled him with the spirit of God, in wisdom, and in understanding, and in knowledge, and in all manner of workmanship, to devise cunning works, to work in gold, and in silver, and in brass, and in cutting of stones, to set them, and in carving of timber, to work in all manner of workmanship. And I, behold, I have given with him Aholiab, the son of Ahisamach, of the tribe of Dan: and in the hearts of all that are wise hearted I have put wisdom, that they may make all that I have commanded thee.

These men were filled with the Spirit of God to design artistic works, to carve wood, to cut jewels, and to work "in all manner of workmanship"! Beware of over-categorizing or boxing in believers based on questionnaire results or even lists compiled from New Testament passages. Leave room for all kinds of gifts and abilities to be utilized for the building up of the kingdom, just as they were for the building of the tabernacle.

God will also ask His followers to demonstrate gifts other than those in which they are endowed. An example is giving. God commands all of His followers to give, but only some of His followers are gifted with the spiritual gift of giving. It is freeing to understand that, while I am required to give, I may not have the all-encompassing inner compulsion to give. This knowledge frees the believer not from responsibility, but from self-imposed guilt.

In a Nutshell

Understanding spiritual gifts means knowing that the God of all has chosen to work through His people. Spiritual giftedness is not as much about what a person can do as how God works through the believer. It is how Christ followers are becoming one with Him rather than merely doing acts of service for Him. When believers express themselves through their particular gifts, they express their faith by demonstrating God's supernatural powers. It is humbling and poignant to experience powerful ministry.

Learning to Listen
Monty Waldron

Before you begin skimming this chapter, I need you to think about something. I want you to imagine that the lives of your family and friends are dependent upon your grasp of the material you are about to read. Imagine that when your eyes pass over the final word, you will be whisked away to a small, enclosed room where you will complete a thorough examination of your comprehension. Your score will determine whether or not the people you love most survive. Now hold on to that image and consider how those circumstances would affect your approach to the content. Would you read it like any other book? Would you make any adjustments to what just comes naturally as your eyes fall on the page? I am going to go out on a limb here and guess that you would read very slowly … carefully … attentively. If it were me, I would suck the marrow out of every word.

Motivation is a curious thing. Raise the stakes on even the most mundane of activities, and we engage at a whole new level. We respond with urgency at the point where need and desire collide. I hope that by the end of this section your need and desire for authentic, life-changing relationships will compel you to listen for the rest of your life like someone's life depended on it. In actuality, there may be few other skills more life giving than the art of listening. Our problem is that we rarely see immediate consequences of poor listening. Nothing seems to be at stake in a single conversation, so we drift, we interrupt, we dominate, and we overlook the relational erosion taking place right before our eyes. I do not expect you or anyone else to truly listen because I say you should. I do, however, suspect that as you and I become increasingly aware of what is at stake, our motivation to lean in and receive what is being said to us will shoot through the roof.

What Is at Stake?

First of all, poor listening undermines our ability to experience intimacy. To really listen is to strive for understanding. And where there is understanding, intimacy has a chance to grow. Second, failure to listen hinders us from receiving the wisdom we so desperately need to walk skillfully through life. Third, an unwillingness to listen renders us incapable of responding in helpful ways to the needs of those around us. Finally, and most important, an inability to listen robs us of the abundant life God offers us in relationship with Him. We miss out on the many overtures of love God makes toward us through His word, His Spirit, and His people, and we suffer as a result. Squandering our fundamental and indispensable capacity to listen comes with a great cost to us and to the people who are most dear to us.

One of the ways I check myself is to identify whether my focus is more on what another person is saying, or on what I plan to say when the person is finished speaking. If I am doing the latter, then I have to admit that while I may be hearing, I am not really listening. That may seem like splitting hairs but I find it helpful to make a distinction. Hearing is primarily a function of the ears, listening is a function of the heart. We were created by God to do far more than perceive the sounds of words and phrases. We were meant to grasp meaning and emotion. I have found that when I have this kind of understanding, I am better able to respond in a meaningful way than if I am mostly consumed with my own thoughts.

Strive for Understanding

It can be difficult to achieve understanding. Try as we might, seeing things differently than we see them naturally is a huge stretch. Generally, we like our view of the world and initially question people who claim to see it another way. It is a rare and courageous person who pushes through the fear of alternative perspectives in search of at least grasping where another person is coming from. Keep in mind that I am not talking about undiscerning agreement, just genuine understanding. Those who are able to do this open up channels of communication that simply are not available to those who can do nothing more than state their own perspective.

I have learned this the hard way by failing to let my wife know that I understand what she is telling me before offering my take on a matter. I do this when I am more afraid of losing a battle than I am interested in connecting and growing in our relationship. Experience has taught me that it is not until she feels as though I genuinely understand her that we are able to move toward resolution. I demonstrate understanding (and let her know that I am really listening) by repeating what she has said, and then asking her if I am on track. When I am able to do this, it becomes far easier for her to then receive my perspective (if it is different) and we are able to find common ground. The next time you are in a verbal exchange with someone, try beginning your response with, "So what you're saying is …." Honestly, it is a practical application of Paul's exhortation, "Let nothing be done through strife or vainglory; but in lowliness of mind let each esteem other better than themselves. Look not every man on his own things, but every man also on the things of others" (Phil. 2:3–4).

Ask Good Questions

Another important skill related to effective listening is asking good, clarifying questions. Not only does it show genuine interest, it aids in the process of arriving at accurate understanding. The best synonym I can think of is curiosity. Children are instinctively curious because they have not already formed opinions about most things, and are naturally in an information-gathering mode. We miss out on so many fascinating insights as we get older simply because we stop asking questions. When someone states a thought about something, let that be a cue for you to explore that thought. You can learn a lot about someone by seeking out how and when that thought was formed. Undoubtedly, what people think emerges out of a rich context of experiences and relationships, a storyline just waiting to be discovered.

When asking questions, a good listener is also watching for nonverbal communication. Facial expressions, gestures, and a person's posture can tell you a great deal about what might be going on behind the words. Being sensitive to these physical signposts will help you respond appropriately to excitement, embarrassment, defensiveness, discouragement, and the like. I often, in the course of conversation, will check what I am seeing with the person I am talking to by stating an observation. I am not declaring a fact, but inviting that individual to either affirm or correct what I have perceived. Once again, this communicates that I am present and engaged beyond the mere exchange of words.

Say "Thank You"

A more recent lesson I have been learning about listening has come through my involvement with recovery groups. If you have never attended an Alcoholics Anonymous meeting or something like it, you are missing out on an environment that is beautifully unique and refreshing. I have personally participated in a group called the Samson Society, and our sharing time has expanded my understanding of communication in profound ways. I now believe that simply saying "thank you" is a powerful response to someone who has been courageous enough to tell the truth about himself. We are conditioned in Christian circles to respond in conversation with advice and clichés. We assume that what people need most is a timely insight, when in reality that may not be the case. Now before you take me to task, I know there are certainly occasions where instruction, correction, or admonition is in order. I am simply suggesting that this is not always the case. One very obvious illustration is the wife who says to her husband, "I don't need a solution, I just need you to listen." If we are truly attentive to people and to the Holy Spirit, I think we will find that many times, God will speak most powerfully through simple appreciation for what has been said.

Why Is Listening So Important?

When doing premarital counseling, I will always ask a couple what they think their greatest motivation will be for listening to each other. I explain that what has motivated me most to listen to my wife is the likelihood that I will ultimately hear from God. I assume that if the Holy Spirit indwells my wife and me, and if He loves me more than I can completely comprehend, I can confidently assume He will want to speak to me through the words of my spouse. God can speak through anyone at any time. I assume that God wants to communicate with me, and that He can use every interpersonal conversation I have to do so. This makes the practice of listening all the more important. In any given dialogue, I have the potential of receiving word from my heavenly Father. What better reason could there be for listening well?

Preparing Members for Change
Monty Waldron

The fact that the topic of change is among those included in this book should tell us something. If we are honest, we know that change is difficult for just about everyone. Even those who are more tolerant of change resist it unless compelled somehow to make it. We are naturally creatures of habit who cling to what is familiar. If you are not convinced of this, take a quick inventory of your own life over the last year. How much tangible, lasting change have you experienced (other than change that was circumstantially forced upon you)? If you are a leader, you are possibly quite resistant to change except that which you initiate. This is important to keep in mind as we think about the prospect of leading others through change.

Personally Embrace Change

Nothing will determine our ability to prepare the people we lead for change than our own willingness to embrace change as a way of life. You have undoubtedly heard the adage: "You cannot take someone where you haven't already traveled." If we as leaders have not come to terms with our need for ongoing change, we will find it very difficult to help others navigate such intimidating terrain. I am deeply indebted to leaders in my life who introduced me to the idea that my relationship with God is a lifelong, life-changing journey that will not be completed until I take my last breath.

Theologically, this is the concept of sanctification, a gracious process of transformation engineered by God to conform us to the image of Jesus Christ, a process He is committed to completing in the lives of all who know him (Phil. 1:6). One of the most beautiful descriptions made of us is that of God's "workmanship" (lit., God's "poem"; Eph. 2:10). Our heavenly Father is perpetually guiding us to ever-greater maturity and inviting us to willingly follow His lead. The more we personally embrace change as a way of life, the more our lives will truly change, and the better able we will be to help others do the same.

Communication Is Key

Whether the change we are envisioning is for individuals or a group, communication is crucial. Some of my greatest failures as a leader have come when I assumed far too much in terms of change-related understanding and desire. As I mentioned earlier, change is not something we naturally pursue until prompted to do so. I cannot expect the people I lead to read my mind nor cooperate with recommended change without healthy dialogue. It would be a grave mistake to simply announce change without making room for questions and feedback.

I have actually found that our congregation is very willing to follow and even make significant adjustments, but they need the opportunity to catch up with the thinking I have already been doing. It is unreasonable for us as leaders to expect people who care about the welfare of our church community to adopt significant changes without inquiry. I assume that my job as a leader is to prayerfully envision a desirable future (which will always require change of some kind) and initiate conversations about the adjustments we will need to make in order to see that future become a reality.

As a catalyst for change, I have found that the better I can anticipate questions and concerns around potential direction, the more confidence I will cultivate in the hearts of the people I serve. This does not mean I must have an immediate answer for every question. It means that I must demonstrate a willingness to thoughtfully explore the recommended path prior to presenting it to the body. To do this, I take time to consider the spiritual, relational, missional, and organizational implications of moving in a new direction. I strive to hear what I plan to communicate with fresh ears, ears that have no prior understanding of what is being heard. This helps me to clarify and quantify the proposal in concrete terms with as few assumptions as possible.

When charting new direction or entering new territory, we need to be able to describe how proposed changes will tangibly affect us (our priorities, calendar, pocketbook, etc.). In addition, we need to honestly describe as best we can the cost and risk associated with adopting or rejecting change of some kind. Avoid the temptation to manipulate at this stage by exaggerating your assessment. Scrutinize your view of the situation from an oppositional perspective. While presenting, genuinely address the vulnerabilities that are out of your control, speak to concerns expressed by your congregation, and commit yourself to following up in the areas that remain unclear.

Vision Casting

If your church members are going to follow you through seasons of change, they must have some idea of where you intend on taking them. They must have a picture of their destination. Simply said, people need vision. I use that word hesitantly, because it has been so distorted. Vision is not just the opinion of the strongest personality in the room. It is not always the most elaborate or spectacular idea presented. It is not necessarily the most radical path available. Biblical vision depicts a future primarily in terms of how God's glory might be displayed as a result of following a particular course of action. Vision describes in detail the God-honoring results of Spirit-led activity. What we call vision needs to be more than a building, a program, or a strategy. We need to convey the potential fruit our activities are intended to produce. We cannot control the results of our efforts—that is God's domain—but we can prayerfully strive after the Spirit-induced, transformational results God delights to produce in the lives of broken people. By the way, God is just as interested in changing broken people inside the church as He is changing those outside the church, leaders included.

When casting vision, I try not to confuse what I consider to be a preferable future with what God prescribes as a preferable future. These are not necessarily mutually exclusive, but there can be a great divide between the two, particularly during difficult circumstances. A classic illustration of this is found in John 11. When Lazarus became ill, Mary and Martha called for Jesus and assumed that his love for their family would compel him to heal Lazarus. This was their preferable future. But when Jesus allowed Lazarus to die, Mary and Martha had to come to terms with a future they initially thought inconceivable. Jesus did not act at all in the way they expected, especially in light of the deep love they knew Jesus had for them. They assumed Jesus would automatically order his priorities solely around their immediate needs. They would later learn that God's glory was priority; it was the determinative factor in a preferable future. Jesus wanted their belief anchored, not in a God who would simply give them what they wanted, but in a God who would give them what they most needed.

Commit to Prayer

We as leaders must lead with vision that orbits around God's purposes, not our preferences. Ideally, our preferences should be aligned with God's purposes. To do this, scripturally informed prayer is essential. Any vision we as pastors propose should bear the unmistakable marks of God's heart to save the lost and equip the found. There is no better way to discover this than in prayerful reflection over the contents of God's word. The time we invest in this way allows us to passionately call our congregations to even the most radical expressions of change.

Utilize Navigational Reference Points

As we forge ahead into the future God has for us, navigational reference points are extremely helpful. Two of the most basic guides I have sought to have in place throughout my ministry are a mission statement and a list of core values. These in no way supersede the Scriptures in terms of authority, but have actually emerged from the Scriptures as a crystallization of broad biblical priorities. They reflect the Great Commission (Matt. 28), the Great Commandment (Mark 12), and the distinct attributes of the church from its first-century founding.

When presenting directional adjustments to the body, we always connect the path we are proposing with our mission and values. In the congregation I am a part of, we believe our mission is to exalt Jesus Christ as a worshiping community of influence by engaging our world with genuine spiritual life. Undergirding this mission are five core values: faith, worship, community, spiritual maturity, and stewardship. These distinctives create a safe, conversational environment where we can passionately explore methodological changes without fear of compromising our identity as the body of Christ.

Commit to Unity

Perhaps the greatest preparation for change we can give the people we lead is a firm commitment to unity.

God delights in it (Ps. 133), Jesus prayed for it (John 17), and it is a key feature of our maturity in Christ (Eph. 4). Where unity is cultivated fruitfulness follows. Where it is neglected, our labor is in vain. Practically speaking, our leadership team embraces unity as nonnegotiable. We consider unanimity to be the primary indicator that we are to proceed with a course of action. Where we disagree we assume that we have not yet arrived at the path God has for us. At times this is less efficient, but preserving unity has proved to build immense trust among our leaders, which actually makes for productive conflict and a strong collective IQ. A commitment to unity amid proposed change validates the importance of our relationships and promotes the pursuit of mutual understanding. With that kind of atmosphere, change presents an exciting opportunity to enter and experience new chapters of our story.

Mentoring and Discipleship
Steffron T. James

And Jesus came and spake unto them, saying, All
power is given unto me in heaven and in earth.
Go ye therefore, and teach [Greek: mathēteusate,
"make disciples of"] all nations, baptizing them in
the name of the Father, and of the Son, and of the
Holy Ghost: Teaching them to observe all things
whatsoever I have commanded you: and, lo, I am
with you always, even unto the end of the world.
Amen.
                                    —Matthew 28:18–20

Could it be that Jesus summarized the ultimate goal
of His entire thirty-three years on earth into four little
words? Go! Make! Baptize! Teach! I believe that, in the
passage above, Jesus communicated the way to be truly
like Him on the earth. Jesus is mentoring disciples, and
in turn asking them to mentor others. Although the word
mentoring does not appear in this passage, I believe it is
implied for those who were to "go." Depending on your
background, a number of terms may be more recognizable to you than *mentor*: spiritual father, provisional
relationship, life coach, guide, or leader. At its simplest,
mentoring is coming into an accountable relationship to
help someone grow. The word *disciple* is used in the reference text. Let us dive into these four last instructions of

Jesus and see what we learn about the relationship of the mentor and disciple.

Go!

"Go therefore" implies the noun *you*. But to whom is *you* referring? Is it just the Eleven on the mountain with Jesus or, as I indicated previously, anyone who answers the call to "go"? A quick observation of the text clarifies it. Jesus directed the Eleven to the nations and promised He would be with them until the end of the age. The Eleven did not reach all nations; they have been dead for more than 2,000 years and time has not ended. So the instructions must be to any person who reads and heeds. But the person giving the instructions is not just any person; He is someone I would call a mentor.

There is some seasoning or life learning that has taken place before a person is called to be a mentor. I want to caution at this point: age can be but is not always a criterion when it comes to being a mentor. When Jesus said to go, He was talking to those who at least were in a position to lead others without falling into in a ditch. Here are a few basic traits that one must have in order to be considered a spiritual mentor:

1. Have soundness of character, and be able to endure difficulty and respond right.

2. Be mature and have self-control.

3. Be disciplined by being consistent in the

Word, prayer, fellowship, worship, and servant life.

4. Be under authority and have his or her own mentor.

5. Manifest fruit of the spirit.

6. Serve as an example by living a life for others to follow.

I believe 2 Timothy 2:2 is the best New Testament verse on this entire process of mentoring/discipleship. Paul tells Timothy, "And the things that thou hast heard of me among many witnesses, the same commit thou to faithful men, who shall be able to teach others also." Learn from someone, teach someone, watch the taught person teach others. Duplication through relationship— is that not the life of Jesus?

Make!

Make disciples of all nations. *You* is understood again—you being a "maturing disciple," a mentor, who accepts the call of Christ. Make others what you are! The Greek verb "to become a disciple" is mathēteuō; it primarily means to be a pupil. Why would you want to be considered a pupil? We have to become a student of what Jesus is like and what He likes. The secondary meaning is to become a follower. It means to mimic or discipline yourself to be just like Him. As we mimic Him (Christ), others will mimic us.

Mimicking Christ does not happen overnight. It will take a time investment. Mentor/disciple connections exist and draw life from each other. What does it mean to invest as a mentor?

1. Humbly realize you have something to offer to others.

2. Realize someone invested himself or herself to teach you; now you teach others.

3. Seek Holy Spirit guidance for the right mentoring opportunities.

4. Be willing to give your life away to serve others.

5. Be willing to let your life be on display as a model for others to follow.

6. Display patient perseverance with the maturing and discipleship process.

What are the characteristics of a disciple?

1. Be teachable and childlike (Matt. 18:3–4; 2 Tim. 3:15–17; Heb. 5:12–14).

2. Do not be a lone ranger; need others (1 Cor. 12:18–21; Eph 4:11–13).

3. Be faithful (Luke 16:10–12).

4. Show willingness to sacrifice (Rom. 12:1–2).

5. Commit long-term to becoming a disciplined one (Phil. 3:14).

We are commanded to go for a reason: to make disciples. Disciples need mentors. Mentors need disciples. Our Lord needs both to fulfill the mandate of having His authority extended throughout the earth.

Baptize!

The word *baptize* is baptizō in Greek. It means to wash or dip in water, to submerge. Matthew 28:19 could be stated, "Our job is to submerge every people group into the Father, Son, and Holy Spirit"; some may say "to get them lost in God." Would that be fulfilling Jesus' original intent if we could all say "I have disappeared and all that is left is God"?

Jesus said, "That they all may be one; as thou, Father, art in me, and I in thee, that they also may be one in us: that the world may believe that thou hast sent me" (John 17:21).

Our being in Him is the best chance of Him flowing out through us as a light to the world. Which is more like Him? To be baptized in the name of the Father, Son, and Holy Spirit and never change one bit? Or to immerse individuals in all that God and His name represents as we experience His fullness, His presence, His love, and His power? Baptizing is more than an act performed once after you acknowledge Jesus' lordship of your life; it is a daily conversion and transformation experience with the Godhead.

Teach!

Go! Make! Baptize! Teach! Why would Jesus have placed *teach* at the end of the list of expectations and instructions? Is this accidental or did our Lord lay a pattern for us to follow even today? First, He told the maturing disciples to go. Then He told them to find those willing to be taught. After pulling together that group, He got them to experience a life-changing relationship with God. Only after following these steps laid out by Jesus will the mentor begin to teach others to observe the commandments. Jesus knew that everything flows out of and is connected with a life-giving relationship with God. Teaching follows maturing, relationship, and a God experience.

Take a look at 2 Timothy 2:24–26:

> And the servant of the Lord must not strive; but be gentle unto all men, apt to teach, patient, in meekness instructing those that oppose themselves; if God peradventure will give them repentance to the acknowledging of the truth; And that they may recover themselves out of the snare of the devil, who are taken captive by him at his will.

Are we really God's representatives (servants)? If so, the following from these three verses should be understood by us.

Verse 24: There are minimum requirements to be one of God's effective servants.

1. Be peacemakers: We are not to be in conflict.

2. Be gentle: Show temperance when dealing with others.

3. Be able or ready to teach: Stay alert to opportunities to bring instruction when needed, warranted, and when requested.

4. Be patient: Show a calm demeanor in trying times and with trying people.

5. Be humble: Have a proper estimation of who you are.

6. Correct wrong actions: But correct these actions only in humility as the person's intercessor.

Verse 25: God really can use us to help others.

1. Realize their opposition is not to the one mentoring.

2. Only God can and does grant repentance; we can help the person seek this repentance.

3. We become the intercessors and instruments for breaking Satan's hold on others.

4. By demonstrating a right attitude and response, we open the door of truth to others.

Verse 26: Results happen for servants (mentors) who act upon the Great Commission.

1. Many of the lost will be saved. Some people in opposition to the gospel will turn to God through hearing the gospel.

2. The person escapes the traps and snares of Satan.

3. Right actions contribute to destroy the influence of the powers of darkness. Satan can no longer use the person for evil.

4. The person is now a ready pupil, and is ready to be discipled in the ways of God.

Will you allow the instructions of Christ to bring conviction to your spirit—that the world may know the Father through your mimicking the life of Christ? I say to you, Go! Make! Baptize! Teach! Let the mentor/disciple relationship transform you into the image of Jesus on earth, amen.

Part Four
Strategy

Live and Teach the Gospel
The "Romans Road" to Salvation

As church leaders, the most important things you can do are to live and to teach the gospel—and those are not mutually exclusive. The "Romans Road" to salvation is a set of tremendously powerful verses paired with explanations of the gospel. Carry this manual with you until you have memorized it. Meditate on its truths and live them out in your own life. Share with others the deep simplicity of the gospel of Christ.

1. Romans 3:23:

   "For all have sinned, and come short of the glory of God." Because all of us have sinned, we are separated from God. Not many people will dispute that they have sinned. We all have personal weaknesses and personal guilt. People are naturally self-serving. Even though people do good things, we all have done our share of wrong.

2. Romans 6:23:

   "For the wages of sin is death; but the gift of God is eternal life through Jesus Christ our Lord." The consequence of our sin is death. This verse explains one of the most important concepts of the Bible in one sentence. God is holy and perfect, without any wrong.

He cannot be in the presence of sin. Because we have all sinned, we are all separated from Him. This is much like a limb being cut from a tree; it has been removed from its source of life. We cannot have spiritual life because we have been removed from God because of sin. So if we have all sinned, and God cannot be in the presence of sin, how can we be saved from eternal spiritual death?

3. Romans 5:8:

"But God commendeth his love toward us, in that, while we were yet sinners, Christ died for us." The penalty for our sin was paid by Jesus Christ. Notice that this verse does not say "God loved us so much that He was really distressed that we were separated from Him by our sin." No! God demonstrated His love. He did something in history that proved His love; Jesus Christ died for us. Despite our sinful condition, Christ died for us. This is the wonderful message of the gospel: God loves us despite our sinful condition, so much that He became a man, Jesus Christ, the perfect, holy, and sinless God in the form of man. He came to die in our stead, taking the penalty of our sins (death) on Himself so that we might live the way God intended for us to live: in total dependence on Him and in total obedience to Him.

4. Romans 10:9:

> "That if thou shalt confess with thy mouth the Lord Jesus, and shalt believe in thine heart that God hath raised him from the dead, thou shalt be saved."

If we repent of our sinfulness, then confess and trust Jesus Christ as the Lord and Savior of our lives, we will be saved from the penalty of sin. The gospel offers us a promise, to save us from the penalty of sin; we must believe it. The gospel also offers us a person, Jesus Christ, who paid our penalty and who deserves to be Lord of our lives; we must receive Him. I would like to invite you right now to pray to God, telling Him you are ready to trust Christ to save you from the penalty of sin and to confess Him as the Lord over your life. There is a prayer you can pray right now, but let the words be your own; do not just repeat words as if they were a spiritual chant, but speak them to the personal God who loves you enough to die for you. "Lord, I admit that I have sinned and made myself unclean before you, the Holy God. I understand that I deserve death as the penalty for my sins, and I believe that Jesus Christ paid this price with His blood. I want to turn away from my life-style of selfishness and sin; I repent. I confess

Jesus Christ as my Savior and I put Him in control of my life as my Lord. I pray in Jesus' name, amen."

Leading a Small-Group Bible Study
Debra Moore

Small groups are excellent structures for any church leader to disciple other believers. A Sunday morning service is almost always structured around a pastor sharing with his congregation. This portion of the service is one-sided simply because the preacher does all the talking. However, a small-group study can provide a time for interaction, feedback, questions, and involvement.

A small study can be an effective way of identifying and training other potential leaders. One of the most important goals of small groups should be delegating responsibility so that future leaders can surface. Every aspect of the group study can be delegated to responsible attendees as the Lord directs. We see Jesus using this form of discipling with his inner circle—the twelve disciples. He had one serving as the keeper of the money. When He went through Samaria and met the woman at the well, He had delegated to His disciples the task of going to the city for food (John 4). Jesus looked for opportunities to assign tasks to His disciples, molding them into leaders who would carry on His work.

Lay Down Ground Rules

It is important in developing a small study group to lay down some ground rules. I usually do this at the first meeting. Here are ten points to emphasize.

1. Pray during the week, asking the Lord to speak to the leader and asking Him to prepare everyone's heart for the meeting.

2. To get the most out of this study, read the Scripture chapter or the book each week and do any homework assignments.

3. Be prompt each week. Make a special effort to be on-site for the icebreaker events. As we all get to know one another, we will feel more comfortable interacting with the group.

4. Practice the principles from Matthew 18 in all relationships with the other group members.

5. Any personal items shared in the group need to stay in the group. If something must be told, contact the person who shared and ask permission. This includes sharing with spouses who may not be present.

6. Remember that everyone is important to the success of the group. The leader alone cannot make this group successful. Most people attend a study not because of the teacher, but because they feel loved and valued.

7. Only one person talks at a time.

8. Everyone participates and no one dominates.

9. Exercise spiritual gifts with the members of the study. For example:

a. Encourage—Contact others during the week as the Lord leads and encourage them. You can call, send cards, or use any method to stay in touch.

b. Serve—When someone expresses a need, ask if you can help him or her.

c. Be Merciful—If someone is hurting, hurt with her or him.

d. Heal—Pray for others' physical or emotional healing.

10. Love! Love! Love! Love! Love! Love! Love!

Since I emphasize everyone arriving on time for the study, it is vital that the leader actually does start the meeting promptly. There should be a time to close the meeting. Except under circumstances where the Spirit of God moves the group to continue, the meeting should adjourn on time.

It is better to limit the study to a specific number of weeks rather than making it an open-ended study. People find it easier to commit to a specific number of weeks than to think they are committing to an indefinite Bible study. You can always extend the study if the group agrees. The more you can let the group be involved in setting the time and the number of weeks, the more likely they are to attend regularly because they have taken some ownership of planning the group study.

Icebreakers—Beginning the Study

Beginning with an icebreaker event is a great way to get people to arrive on time. We all like to have fun. The leader needs to make sure that the icebreakers are so appealing that folks want to come early to participate in them. A good leader will look often for a creative person to conduct the icebreakers each week. Icebreakers not only help people arrive on time, they help the people learn to know and appreciate one another. They set the mood for involvement and participation right at the beginning of the study.

There are countless ideas for starting a meeting. By doing an Internet search on *icebreakers*, the person responsible for this aspect of the meeting can get almost unlimited ideas like these:

1. Pass around a bowl of M&Ms and have each person grab some. The number of M&Ms a person takes is how many facts about himself or herself the person has to share with the group.

2. Ask a question and go around the room asking everyone to answer. Examples: Was there ever a time when you questioned whether God existed? Who is the most important person in your life other than your spouse? Why?

3. Have each person write down two truths about herself or himself and one lie. Let the others guess which item is a lie.

4. Set up teams of five. Each team will receive one pair of new garden gloves and one pack of gum (five pieces per pack). When the group leader says "go," the first person in each team is to put on the garden gloves, open the package of gum, pull out a piece, unwrap it, chew it, and then pass the gloves and the pack of gum to the next person. The first team to complete the task wins.

5. Lay lots of items in a tray for viewers to see and have participants pass the tray around. Remove the tray from sight and have participants list what was on the tray. The person who lists the most objects is the winner. You can give extra points or break ties by asking specific questions like "What flavor was the sucker?" and so on.

6. Toward the end of the study, go around the room and ask everyone to encourage one another by sharing what one thing comes to mind when someone's name is mentioned.

Teaching—The Meat of the Study

After the icebreaker is complete, the leader should make a transition to the teaching time. This can be done in a number of ways like having someone lead in singing some songs, having a time of prayer, or going over some homework. Remember that one of the goals of a small group is to identify and train other leaders. A secure, effective leader will choose others to be in charge of the transition time.

The teaching time is normally the meat of the study. However, the leader should not be surprised if the Holy Spirit moves through one of the other times such as the icebreaker, worship, or the prayer time. The leader must allow the Holy Spirit to do His work in His way.

Many American believers have lost a commitment to the promise that the Word of God can change lives. But God's Word must always be the centerpiece of every study: "For the word of God is quick, and powerful, and sharper than any twoedged sword, piercing even to the dividing asunder of soul and spirit, and of the joints and marrow, and is a discerner of the thoughts and intents of the heart" (Heb. 4:12).

There are a number of principles that a leader should observe as he prepares to teach a Bible study.

1. Be prepared through prayer and personal study. Do not let the preparation rob you of your personal time with the Lord.

2. Be enthusiastic. When I taught as a Bible college professor, my students bought me a T-shirt that said, "Enthusiasm is contagious. Let's have an epidemic." Allow the attendees to see your passion for the Word of God. Share personal experiences to show the living power of the Word.

3. Be sensitive to the moving of the Holy Spirit. There is a balance between maintaining order in the study and quenching the Holy Spirit.

4. Encourage questions. The small-group setting is the best place for people to get immediate feedback to their questions. If you do not know the answer, always feel free to say, "That's a great question. I'd like to think about it for next week if that is good with you." Do not forget to study and answer it the next week.

5. Value input from others. No one is too insignificant to participate. No attendee is more important than any other. One of my favorite songs has a very sobering line: "The ground is even at the foot of the cross."

6. Adapt the study at each meeting. Flexibility is vital for a good leader. If a leader gets set in his ways, he may miss what the Lord really wants to do in that session. Have your prayer team pray for discernment and flexibility for you.

7. Apply the principles of the Word or study to the lives of people. Ask the Lord to teach you the lessons of the study personally before you try to teach them to the group. A message prepared in the head reaches the head. A message prepared in the heart reaches the heart.

Prayer and Ministry Time—
Ending the Study

A true leader will "rejoice with them that do rejoice, and weep with them that weep" (Rom. 12:15). Jesus empathized with the needs of people. The prayer and ministry time is crucial because it gives people an outlet for the problems they face. Nothing can affect a person like having other believers gather around to pray for her or him. One week the leader might say, "How can we pray for each of you in regards to what was taught today?"

This presents another opportunity for the leader to find someone with leadership potential to conduct this phase. This person could ask particular people to pray or just have a time of prayer where he closes. Conversational prayer is a favorite of many people. There may be times when a person needs so much encouragement that attendees may want to actually lay their hands on his shoulders. The leader could ask for volunteers to remember specific prayer requests during the week. It would be awesome if someone remembered a particular prayer request and called that person during the week to ask how things are going. Now that would build relationships and give encouragement!

Most of all, remember to report each answered prayer to the group so that everyone is encouraged as God moves in response to prayer.

Small study groups can change the hearts of people. They are effective because everyone needs to be loved and appreciated. Small groups offer a setting where interaction and attention can be given to individuals. People will come to small groups who will not darken the doors of a church. There are thousands of individuals—believers included—who have been hurt by the church and refuse to go. Small groups can be a way to reach out to them and help heal wounds and restore hope.

The actions of Jesus Himself show us the importance of small groups. He chose twelve men to disciple. He let them walk with Him. He let them ask questions. He spent time praying for them. He got to know them and their families personally. He saw their potential and knew that He wanted to leave the spread of the gospel in their hands. Yes, He is the prime example of investing in a small group of people. Perhaps He would say to us, "Go and do likewise."

Preservice/In-service Training

Yvonne E. Thigpen

Mission Critical Training

As the first decade of the new millennium unfolded into "The Great Recession," the consequential disequilibrium caused church leaders at all levels to rethink their mission, particularly with regard to church educational programs. The critical assessment was long overdue and present-day strategies must incorporate that fact into their training tactics.

Clearly, God's strategy for His followers is that they be able to teach. Additionally, He expects the teaching to be replicated in a manner that allows those taught to teach others. The command is straightforward and clear. Our execution, however, is often complex and confusing only because we fail to link it appropriately to the overall strategy of our mission. All church leaders have the biblical responsibility for nurturing and equipping church members for ministry. Parachurch organizations might help the church with dual goals and resources, but it is the primary responsibility of the church working through its leadership.

Measuring a leader's effectiveness is an important leadership function. Jesus taught this principle many times in the New Testament. Several of His parables stressed this truth (i.e., Matt. 21:33–36; 25:14–30; Luke 12:47–48). Paul also told Timothy that how well he developed others was a strong indication of his own leadership. Paul carefully explained we must use great care in selecting, nurturing, and equipping each person placed into church ministry (1 Tim. 5:21, 22). Finally, Paul told Timothy that his future evaluation by God depended upon how effective he was in developing others (2 Tim. 4:8).

Linking Relationship to Equipping Strategy

Nurturing (discipling) and equipping (training) church leaders are not mutually exclusive goals.[4] Paul instructed Timothy that all Scripture was inspired by God and "profitable for doctrine, for reproof, for correction, for instruction in righteousness: That the man of God may be perfect [nurtured to maturity], thoroughly furnished [ready to serve Christ] unto all good works" (2 Tim. 3:16–17). God's Word stresses that both nurture and equipping should be treated together as a dual goal in the believer's life.

The trend in many churches of the late twentieth century, and carried into the present dilemma, is to emphasize personal discipleship (which stresses the development of the inner man) at the expense of helping the person discover and employ his or her spiritual gifts to serve Christ in his world. Yet the Scriptures continually link the two saying that nurture should result in equipping believers to serve. In 1 Thessalonians 2:7, Paul stresses caring and gentleness, and concluded by describing a caring ministry for others. Therefore, since the Bible links nurture and equipping, it is also necessary to associate the two when evaluating the equipping strategy for church leaders. In concert, nurture focuses on developing individual believers to discover, claim, and be all that their Creator designed them to be, while equipping focuses on developing believers to minister efficiently and effectively in their world.

The Selection Process

Such an important mission logically suggests a means for selection and assessment for the task ahead. A church leader must first understand the personality and environment of his current ministry situation in order to determine how best to assess, recruit, and assign workers.

The late Dr. Kenn Gangel shared a timeless checklist in his work *Biblical Leadership*,[5] prefaced by his lifelong mantra "Recruitment *follows* assessment." It is imperative that the ministry worker be fit for a spiritual task with certain identifiable characteristics. Gangel's checklist includes:

1. Christlikeness—becoming more like Christ each year in one's attitudes, words, and actions

2. Character—who a person is when nobody is watching

3. Competence—the ability to do the task

4. Charisma—being someone with an outgoing, welcoming, or friendly personality

5. Communication skills—someone who can explain or write things understandably

6. Compatibility—being adaptable to others, especially with existing team members

7. Coachability—being eager and willing to improve

8. Commitment—showing loyalty and a willingness to follow through with the church, other team members, or that particular ministry

Second, a church leader should identify a spiritual gifts assessment. Your pastoral staff will likely have either theological or theoretical preferences for how to go about selecting an assessment tool. Much like wrapping our minds around the mission relationship of equipping to training, it is also important not to diminish the giftedness of individuals when preparing them for service. There is purposeful assessment during boot camp exercises that determine the appropriateness of later placement. The most horrific woundedness of spiritual soldiers comes when the tyranny of the urgent overtakes prudent, nurturing judgment among leaders. Find a spiritual gift assessment process that is both compatible with biblical foundations and serves your particular ministry mission.

Finally, with a clear Christlike attitude toward service being evident, and spiritual gifts being identified, a basic understanding of learning styles is helpful for success in the training process. The study of learning styles is important because it can help us discover how we as teachers learn, how students (or teams) will learn, and what will be the most effective methodologies to utilize in the training process:

1. Does your volunteer learn best independently or would he or she benefit from a group orientation?

2. Will your volunteer function best with serialized training sessions or can you rely on a comprehensive event?

3. Does the volunteer absorb training information best by reading on his or her own, observing a ministry in action, or participating in a mentorship?

In today's world the church leader will quickly realize the pool of volunteers represents all learning styles, so multiple communication and training venues are appropriate.

Training Is a Tactical Process

No army of any worth would grab recruits off the street and throw them into the heat of battle without adequate evaluation, training, and appropriate resources. Once the church leader has prepared a foundation for spiritual nurture and equipping the volunteer, and bolstered her or his confidence with a spiritual gift assessment, it is time to train that worker for a specific task. Remember:

1. Equipping identifies and develops an individual's potential; training develops proficiency.

2. Equipping teaches problem solving; training teaches technique.

3. Equipping often begins a new ministry; training generally maintains existing ministry.

4. Equipping focuses on the goal; training focuses on the task.

Up to this point all efforts have targeted preservice assessments and training. In-service training involves assembling the right recruits for the task and proceeds to arm them with skills and resources to accomplish the specific goals. What then should the arsenal include?

Establish an expectation for Bible study skills being nonnegotiable in active service. Provide either the information for acquiring these skills or the actual Bible study tools for your volunteers. Some churches house these resources at a church library or learning resource center. More commonly today, individuals acquire their own personal aids in a delivery system that suits their personal preferences. Technology now enables everyone with accessible and user-friendly Bible study aids that do not require formal seminary degrees. Electronic libraries, with packaged study aids, do much of the professorial work for the individual, leaving a digestible portion for rapid learning. Mobile device applications can travel with us wherever we go. For the traditionalists, print editions are available and hundreds of Bibles are published with the essential aids built into the margins or appendixes of the text. There is to be no tolerance for sidestepping quality Bible study. Without the sword of God's Word, the battles are already lost.

Develop an expectation and plan for a prayer and meditation discipline. It should be more than a casual suggestion to your team. Like you provide resources for Bible study, provide resources for enhancing prayer life and share specific prayer requests on a regular basis.

Establish a clear purpose for the training with a ministry description. You may want to create a simple, single-purpose card, brochure, or page in a training manual that is handy for participants and clearly states the ministry's purpose, without allowing assumptions. Affirm everyone understands:

1. Why this ministry position exists

2. Who this ministry position reports to

3. What resources are available to help this ministry fulfill its purpose

4. When training will be provided to the person who is in this ministry position

5. What evaluation process will be used and when it will take place

Create a checklist of resources involved with the ministry; flesh out the question of what resources are available. If you are training people to lead a Sunday school class, you will want the chosen curriculum present at the training session to highlight its distinctiveness. If you are training for nursery duty, you may want to provide a tour of the facility and demonstrate practices and procedures. If you are training others for an adult small-group ministry, you may want to invite a seasoned leader to share experiences, options, and advice.

In today's world the business of ministry must be considered without overshadowing the ministry itself. We are obliged to create governing policies, budgets, and counseling. The particular documents and legalities need to be shared for the greater good of ministry sustainability.

Finally, view technology as your strategic friend. Beyond the participant's orientation, not to mention common communication options, many ministries are sustained with wise use of the Internet. You can easily, and economically, allow your church Web site to be a hub for downloading information, forms, or white papers that address frequently needed topics. You can post video clips containing training tips, demonstrations, or highlights. Most important, you can cultivate a culture for training as a regular feature of your leadership.

To summarize, training is not an optional activity for church leaders. Effective leaders will both know for themselves and communicate to their teams that a nurtured spiritual relationship is essential to assess and equip volunteers. The preservice equipping will examine Christlike attributes toward service, identify spiritual gifts, and cultivate an understanding of learning styles. Each in-service training will include essential tactical tools of Bible study skills, prayer and meditation discipline, ministry descriptions, a resource checklist, business of ministry documents, and descriptions of the uses of technology. Training can then be both efficient and effective.

Technology and Ministry
Neil Glotfelty

Today's technologies pervade our lives and ministries, and that's not entirely bad. In fact, never before has the church had such an enormous amount of tools at its disposal to "go ye into all the world, and preach the gospel to every creature" (Mark 16:15). Whether one uses e-mail, blog sites, Web sites, streaming video, Facebook, smartphones, text messaging—the list goes on almost ad infinitum—these techno venues provide churches with a global audience and one of the greatest communications opportunities of all times. If used wisely, a church can go far in fulfilling the Great Commission. But the pervasiveness of technology has a dark side as well. Let me give you three bits of experienced-based wisdom to keep church leaders and their ministries on the straight and narrow.

Bit of Wisdom 1: Do Not Let Technology Take over the Ministry

I realize that this advice sounds obvious, but most ministries are quickly becoming technology dependent. Technology is a fantastic tool, but this dependence can invade every aspect of our daily lives. It begins to consume our attention and energy; instead of making us more effective and connected, it makes us tired, disconnected, and distracted.

Consider this: tools that are intended to help us communicate and stay connected to one another can often drive a social wedge between even the best of colleagues and friends. Instead of growing in real relationships, we develop virtual relationships that consume our time but do little to enrich our lives in Christ. True, we can stay better connected via e-mail and blog sites to friends, family, and ministry colleagues who live far away, but far too often we allow these venues to distract us from healthy and vital face-to-face contact. Hebrews 10:24 reminds us not to forsake our gathering together, for this is where we are stirred up to love and do good works. I am certainly not suggesting that we abandon social networking and technology, but I am suggesting that we use these tools to make new friends or to begin relationships with those who would otherwise not know about our vital ministry to them. Allow these online communities to augment your ministry and enhance it, but not direct it. Do not allow technology to substitute for real relationships.

Technology can also subtly take over your time and attention. I cannot begin to tell you how many prayer meetings, worship services, and Bible studies I have seen interrupted and even hijacked by PDAs and smartphones. In fact, I have been in prayer meetings with groups of pastors who were constantly called away from the prayer time by their cell phones. I understand that all of these calls, text messages, and e-mail are "important," but let me suggest that you put up some needed fences against ill-timed interruptions. You certainly cannot be available all the time. Allow your cell phone or smartphone to empower you to be available more than ever before, but know when to turn it off and when you are simply not available.

Even more pervasive than cell phones and smartphones is e-mail! The very word *e-mail* can conjure up the feeling of being invaded and overwhelmed. E-mail is an important and essential tool, but it also has the ability to distract you from your work and rob you of your time. Never before has someone been able to contact you from anywhere, at any time, to assign you work.

Be careful to limit the amount of time that you spend e-mailing. In fact, do not leave it open throughout the day to interrupt you at any time. Decide when you will and will not read and answer e-mail. Establish a disposable e-mail address that you use for e-commerce and online subscriptions. This will preserve your "real" e-mail address for important and necessary communications. And lastly, do not forget to write with pen and paper. There is nothing so encouraging as writing and receiving a good old-fashioned letter.

Bit of Wisdom 2: Always Maintain the Highest Levels of Technological Integrity

Consider this: how many worship services are conducted with pirated software, music, and videos? Pirating is stealing, and pirates have no place leading a worship service. My advice is this: forget trying to impress and maintain integrity instead! Now I realize that this may be painful, but paying for what you use is the right thing to do. Not only does it protect your ministry and those who serve with you, it gives you and your ministry a unique reputation in a world where piracy is commonplace, but integrity is not.

Technology has created what some call the "gift economy," a place where information, software, and services are given to the end-user for free. The downside of this movement is that we have created a cultural expectation that all software, information, and services are free. As a result, many churches sacrifice integrity for what is believed to be "free technology." While this is a quick way to "empower" your ministry with the latest software or media, this "free" stuff could cost you dearly.

As a church leader it is vital that you set the highest standard here. Be sure that all of the software, music, and multimedia that your church and ministry leaders use is fully licensed to the church. Do not fudge. Fudging in this area not only puts you and your ministry at risk, it also puts all of your ministry workers and their hard work at risk as well. It is better to do without than to use something illegally. Remember, God will provide all of your needs in Christ Jesus—paid for in full.

Now that you have set the standard for maintaining integrity in the technology you use, let us figure out how to pay for it. First, establish a long-range budget. This will give you the time you need to save for new purchases and important upgrades that you will want and need in the future. Second, always take advantage of charity-pricing programs. Almost all software and hardware vendors generously provide charity pricing to churches and nonprofit ministries. In fact, distributors like CCBNonprofits.com provide churches with a single point of contact for purchasing both hardware and software at charity pricing. Lastly, make sure that you keep sufficient control and records over your software licensing and a list of who has access to these programs. Following these simple steps will not only help you establish integrity in technology, it will help you set an example in your community.

Bit of Wisdom 3: Focus on People, Not Technology

Technology always comes with bells and whistles that can make an impressive impact. But these attractive features also have a way of getting all of the attention. Sometimes ministries and their leaders place so much importance on technology that technology becomes the end rather than the means. Technology can eclipse the real vision and mission of the ministry, and low-tech people may feel intimidated and out of place. Instead, guide technology to serve you, the people whom you serve, and those who serve with you. Also, do not abuse your IT guys. Do not put them in compromising positions, and do not let them take the blame for everything that goes wrong. Instead, empower them and invest in them.

When possible, strive for technological independence. I realize that some Internet-based ministries need technology for their very existence, but at least ask yourself these questions, "Am I using a particular type of technology just for the sake of the technology?" "Is it really serving the ministry better, or would a low-tech method accomplish the same result?" "Would allowing more people involvement in the work of the ministry bring a better result?" Putting technology in its rightful place—working behind the scenes to serve the ministry—will honor your people, and when you have the inevitable technology breakdown or glitch, it will not be so painful. It might even be refreshing.

Certainly, technology has entered our ministries with great impact. It has delivered opportunities never before available. But will the impact to your ministry be positive or negative? In truth, it will most likely be a blend of both. Following these three bits of wisdom, however, will help you lessen the negative influence of technology. Instead, allow technology to work for you to achieve the highest results and to have a tremendously positive impact for the glory of God.

How to Lead an Effective Meeting
Ed Jent

The most important aspect of leading a meeting is making sure you are going where the Lord wants you to go. We need marching orders. When you get marching orders it usually signifies one of two things: either you are to take action or it is a notice of dismissal. I usually think about marching orders as the signal to take action. Once a person has marching orders, he or she can take action. The plan has been made, communicated, and it is now your job to carry it through. You have your marching orders.

Spiritually, the problem we encounter is acting before we have marching orders or, in some cases, ignoring the marching orders that have been clearly communicated. Where there is a lack of spiritual maturity or a void of spirituality the problem would be developing your own orders.

David was not immune to marching orders. I love this passage:

> And let it be, when thou hearest the sound of a going in the tops of the mulberry trees, that then thou shalt bestir thyself: for then shall the LORD go out before thee, to smite the host of the Philistines. And David did so, as the LORD had commanded him; and smote

the Philistines from Geba until thou come to
Gazer. (2 Sam. 5:24–25)

David was supposed to wait until he heard literal
marching in the balsam trees. Acting prior to this would
have resulted in defeat.

Walking with the Lord means that we must wait
until we understand what He wants us to do before we
take action. Often we suffer defeat and never stop to
understand that the reason for this is that we took action
without clear direction from Jesus. Want to be in a right
relationship with Jesus? Wait until you get your marching
orders before taking action. But when you do, proceed
as if the victory is yours, because it is. The confidence
you gain from hearing from the Lord will enable you to
lead meetings with confidence. Let us look at a few other
things that will help us be effective.

Agendas

One of the most helpful items a person can have for
a meeting is an agenda. It does little good to determine
what your marching orders are to be if you do not focus
on the important items at hand. Agendas are like fences
keeping the items you want in the room in and the items
that are not priorities out of the room.

Agendas also help you to prepare for a meeting in
a logical fashion. The adage "the good is the enemy of
the best" is true when it comes to meetings. Without an
agenda it is easy to spend a lot of time on items that are

good and miss those that would be the best. Carefully plan your agenda so you can spend time on the "marching orders" that will most help you get to the destination you have determined.

Agendas should be printed and distributed to everyone so they can stay on task. Participants can stay focused if they know that the item(s) they want to discuss are slated. Agendas also help you allot an appropriate amount of time for each discussion.

Leave Meetings with an Action Plan

An effective meeting requires that an action plan is established when the meeting is over. Each person should know what is to be accomplished and who is in charge of each particular task. This process ensures accountability. If you leave a meeting without knowing what is to be accomplished and by whom, you are creating frustration in your organization. Granted, some meetings are designed to communicate information but the point is that all meetings should be started with an end result in mind.

Meeting notes should be taken; as soon as possible after the meeting, they should be typed and distributed to each participant. Once distributed, everyone can read them and determine if they match what was discussed in the meeting. Once the participants agree to the content of the minutes, they can be distributed to other people in the organization. This important step allows people who are in the organization to see what was discussed and move in the direction that has been set.

Create an Environment of Participation

Allowing a person to speak up in meetings is important to your overall success. God uses lots of people to provide the "sounds in the mulberry trees," so take time to listen to those who are working in your ministry. Everyone sitting at the table needs to feel comfortable giving their input. Effective leaders understand that not everyone has the same skill in presenting their ideas. Therefore, great leaders invest energy in decoding or interpreting a person's intent. Your listening skills are a major factor in determining participation and your listening skills are often determined by how well you can interpret the statements of those in your meetings.

Another effective way to create participation is to create an environment that allows participants to fail. I tell people around me on a regular basis that if you do not have at least a few items a year that do not completely bomb out, you are being way too conservative. Do not get me wrong. I am competitive and want to win each and every time, but often you learn more from mistakes than successes.

Promote Additional Two-Minute Meetings

Holding two-minute meetings between scheduled major meetings can ensure success. Two-minute meetings keep ministry on course and save an infinite amount of time by not forcing people to address problems only in major meetings. When we pause along the way to give or gain understanding, we are working smart.

Two-minute meetings are also a sign of a church's health. If people are getting together to work things out on the fly, you can be confident you have an environment conducive to getting ministry accomplished.

Prepare Handouts, Slides, and Charts

One comment I seldom hear is "That meeting didn't last long enough." When we communicate much in a short period of time, we are more effective. Visual aids are a great asset in communicating information and helping people understand. Once during the NBA playoffs it struck me how coaches, during time-outs, have their clipboards out drawing plays so the players can see as well as hear what is to be accomplished.

Problem solving is easiest when you develop a flowchart from beginning to end. Recently, we had a discussion about a guest who would visit the church. We developed a flowchart of what happens to this person from the time he or she drives onto the parking lot until the time he or she drives off. We did this with different sized families and scenarios. We learned how to better utilize our welcome center, greeters, and signage. The conversation also sparked some new ideas about how to follow up.

The time spent outside of a meeting preparing for your meeting is never wasted time. Effective meetings inspire effective work, and inspiration is never created from a lack of preparation. Be prepared and show that you see others' time as valuable. Do not turn your meeting into a group read or evaluation of data. Use your data to bring clarity to your point. Explain why you are showing your data, why it is important, and why it is relevant to the meeting.

Invite the Right People to the Meeting

A key element to leading an effective meeting is inviting the right people to the meeting. Spend time determining who should be there and why. If the group is not accustomed to meeting together, begin by explaining why everyone is there. This will give other participants perspective on who is the recognized authority on different elements of the upcoming discussion.

Invite with delegation in mind. If it is possible to delegate directly from the meeting—and usually it is—others in the meeting also know who is responsible for each category. This enables participants to accomplish their tasks much more effectively. Instead of others placing a call to you, they are able to go to the person directly responsible for that aspect of the project.

The Meeting Leader

When you lead a meeting, keep a healthy balance between focus and fun. Nobody wants to go to a dry, dull, boring meeting but no one wants to attend a meeting where nothing is accomplished either. Do not be scared to pull the meeting back on track with something like, "Sorry guys, I've gotten off track. Let me restate our objective here."

When you are leading a meeting, you are in charge of allocating the time people have the floor. Do not allow a few people to dominate your meeting. Equally important is your responsibility to pull out and present the ideas of those who are not as comfortable speaking in front of groups. Use statements that encourage participants to further unpack their thoughts: "Would you mind elaborating on that thought?" "Could you give me any details you are thinking of concerning (name a particular component of their statement)?"

Meetings do not have to be dreaded or feared. The meeting leader/facilitator is the most important component in this arena. Everyone is looking to you for leadership. Keep your meeting moving toward the fulfillment of assignments and the stated objective and everyone will love you for it.

Meetings are a representation of how we are hearing from the Lord. Evaluate your meeting and you will discover truths about your ministry. Once you hear your marching orders (your vision), schedule your meeting.

Tools of the Trade
Organizational Charts, Ministry Descriptions, and Yearly Goals
Jeff Nichols

A major-league pitcher can throw a baseball ninety miles an hour or faster. Is that the only criterion for determining if that pitcher is a good pitcher? No. That only determines if he has what is required to be a major-league pitcher.

Once he is in the majors a pitcher is rated or evaluated based on what seems like a never-ending series of statistical and analytical categories, with earned run average, win-loss record, and strikeout-to-walk ratio but a few.

A minister at your church has the ability to relate to people and meet their needs. Does that mean he is an effective minister? No. That means he has what is required to be a minister at your church.

Every week, in my role as executive pastor, I have the opportunity to sit down with each of our ministry staff members. The purposes of these meetings are for me to to encourage, evaluate, and receive feedback. How can I give staff members the feedback they need? The encouragement they deserve? The feedback that will make them better ministers? What can I use to measure their effectiveness and progress rather than a subjective feeling I have about their ministry? How can you do this as a leader within your own congregation, whether measuring your own effectiveness or that of others?

I would like to suggest a three-pronged approach in your leadership. This approach has proved to be a valuable asset in leading others to be better ministers and helped me to be a better ministry supervisor.

I have three documents in front of me each time I meet with a leader: the person's ministry description, organizational chart, and yearly goals.

Ministry Descriptions

The purpose of keeping a person's ministry description before us each time we meet is to answer the question: is he or she doing what we hired him or her to do? If the answer is no, there are two possible reactions: we change the ministry description to accurately reflect what he or she is currently doing or we change his or her course to get him or her back in line with what we established as his or her primary responsibilities.

This assumes ministry descriptions are in place for any leadership position, including yours. If not, I would strongly recommend developing ministry descriptions that are true, accurate, and realistic. A ton of resources are available online so you do not have to start from scratch.

A good ministry description should list basic functions; describe working relationships, specifying those people he or she is responsible to and those he or she is responsible for; outline gifts and skills needed; and list specific responsibilities. Make each of these areas as specific as you need them to be. Remember, it is a working document, not a dead one that will reside in a folder then be forgotten.

Organizational Chart

A potential roadblock to your church's potential growth can be a lack of organizational integrity in ministry areas. If you have organizational charts sitting in a notebook somewhere, but no one ever refers to them, it makes growth difficult. If your ministries are ministering, but they are unable to handle many more people with the current structure, or lack thereof, it is time to develop more organization.

Church leaders are competent, passionate servants who love people, minister to people, and love ministry. But organizational structure is not necessarily their default setting. Using a very qualified leader in your church who has business and ministry experience can help you get organized. The path can be uncomfortable and hard, but that path can lead eventually to a fully developed, realistic organizational chart serving as an essential tool for evaluation and feedback.

Sure, organizational charts are not exciting. But once your leaders realize laying out their ideal organizational chart can help alleviate some of the myriad responsibilities they personally shoulder, they become excited about charts.

An organizational chart is a graphic illustration of the working relationships described in the ministry description. To whom is this person responsible and for whom is this person responsible?

The question is how do you draw the organizational chart? The way you want it to be or the way it actually is? The answer is both. Start out with the current situation, and then draw the ideal situation. Ideal does not mean unrealistic—the more realistic the better.

Here is an example of how this can work. A new youth pastor realized after starting his job that his current organizational chart had one director or ministry area leader: him. Once he was able to think through the different ministry areas and draw boxes under his, which represented ministry leaders or directors, a load was lifted from him. He set out to recruit those ministry area leaders. When asked how his task of recruiting a key ministry position was coming, he was excited about the potential of a very qualified leader filling that position on his organizational chart. Amazing.

Develop a master organizational chart for the entire church and a more detailed one for each ministry area.

List of Ministry Goals

The third tool I use in regular leader evaluations is a set of ministry-specific goals. These goals determine the specific direction for their ministry area for the next twelve to twenty-four months. The ministry goals are developed over a period of time but specifically written down at our annual fall leadership retreat, which serves as the planning retreat for the next year. The ministry goals that come out of this retreat serve as the basis for our ministry planning.

A few years ago our pastor developed the flowchart on page 173 to illustrate our planning process in relation to our goals:

Two items come to the fore when we plan yearly ministry goals:

1. The Annual Ministry Budget: Every goal, whether a ministry event, promotion, program, or process needs to be funded adequately. All ministry goals are actually shared with our church's finance committee so they can understand the basis of the proposed budgets.

2. Project Planners: As described on the Planning Process flowchart, each goal should have a project planner attached to ensure that the goal is reached. The Project Planner is the daily guide to help the minister achieve the larger goal.

Many tools are available today to help ministers break down their yearly goals into manageable tasks, which then get transferred onto their to-do lists. It is a good idea for church leaders to use at least three different methods to track and manage goals. Any chosen method, system, or program has to be one you are comfortable with and will use.

Order is all around us. Our God is inexplicably creative and effective, neither of which is possible without structure and organization. Are you ready to reflect the glory of our God by getting organized and helping others to do the same?

THE PLANNING PROCESS

EVALUATION

OWNERSHIP ACQUISITION & PROGRAM IMPLEMENTATION

OUR PROGRAM AND PROJECT PLANNING
is the process we use to ensure that our goals are completed. Each significant goal is stated at the top of the page, followed by an implementation chart (or Project Planner). This planner should list all the components of the project (action steps, staffing, budgets, methods, materials, promotions, etc.) listed in a form that will provide visual sequencing.

OUR GOALS
are one-to-two year intentions. They should be SMART: Specific, Measurable, Attainable, Relevant, and Timed.

OUR PROJECTIONS
are the anticipated programs, additions, changes, improvements and innovations that we foresee over the coming five years that will enable us to meet our objectives.

OUR OBJECTIVES
are statements of general intention in a localized area of ministry. They are more specific than mission or vision statements, yet broader than goals. For example: To provide pastoral care for each person in our church.

CREATIVITY

OUR MISSION
is to extend and strengthen the kingdom for Christ and His glory.

OUR VISION
is to provide our area with a growing church blending contemporary style with respect for the traditions of historic Christianity, having a global impact and an evangelistic burden for people of every age and condition. We are committed to be: biblical in our message and means; prayerful in our ministries; innovative in our methodologies; visible in our ministry area and utterly dependent on the Lord Jesus Christ to do what only He can do in the building of his church.

THE NEEDS
of those we serve.

PRAYER

DISCUSSION

"Planning Process Layout," created by Robert J. Morgan; graphic illustration by Stephen L. Fox. Used with permission.

Setting and Enforcing Budgets
Randal D. Ongie

I have seen seminary-trained pastors, caring counselors, gifted church staff members, and servant-hearted
volunteers brought to their knees (pardon the pun) by
one simple statement: "it's time to turn in your budget."
In my years of serving as an executive pastor, and now as
a church consultant, I have yet to meet the first church
staff member who pursued a role in ministry because he
wanted to help establish or manage a ministry fund budget. Budgeting is one of those unpleasant tasks that most
feel ill equipped to engage in and that gives one a sense of
relief when it is completed. Much of this stress is caused
by a lack of understanding about what a budget is and
how it should be approached.

A budget should be defined as a financial plan that
mirrors your ministry plan. The clearer your ministry
plan, the easier it will be to budget. Do not lose sight
of this definition as we move forward. Every ministry
area should have a solid, realistic annual plan that is
approved by the pastor or ministry leadership team. The
plan should be considered based on alignment with the
church's vision and mission and should integrate with all
other ministry efforts for the next ministry year. Once
the plan is approved, each ministry area should simply be
asked to estimate what it will cost. This should be done
item by item to ensure that a good rationale exists for the
total dollars requested. It will also be easier to go back to

make cuts, if necessary, to less essential activities. If cuts are made to the budget, they should also be made to the ministry plan based on your overall ministry priority.

Budget Process

Ministries should use a zero-based budget process. What does that mean? Every budget area should start at zero and be built from there. It does not matter what a ministry area spent last year. Many items are and should be nonrecurring expenses that come and go based on specific plans for that year. This approach should promote innovation and flexibility in planning along with greater ownership and budget adherence.

I always started the budgeting process by giving the staff actual spending summaries for their ministry areas for the previous year. This may seem to work against a zero-based approach, but that was not the intent. Many areas buy similar goods and services year after year and if we provide them with what they actually spent, they have a better chance of accurately predicting what they will need for those same goods or services for the next ministry year.

You might also write some guidelines about how you would like staff members' budget work formatted. Including a copy of their annual ministry plan also helps remind them that they have already done the hard work of planning and simply need to put cost estimates to it. The person charged with coordinating the budget process should offer to meet with each staff member or volunteer at the start of budgeting work to answer questions or clar-ify what has been requested. I also asked that requests for capital equipment (you will need to provide a definition of what you consider capital equipment for your team) be made separately, since I had a separate budget line item and approval process for capital equipment church-wide. You should meet face-to-face with all staff members to receive their budget submissions to be sure they are com-plete and that you fully understand them.

Use of Technology

Software can now economically aid every size church in establishing a budget and tracking actual spending against it. At a minimum, your software should have a budgeting feature. It is also extremely helpful if your reports can be converted to spreadsheets, which can eas-ily be shared electronically. In fact, within a few hours of the end of a month, I was able to use this type of soft-ware to e-mail reports in an easy-to-read format to more than fifty people. You should be able to assign a ministry expense category to every check you write, which will allow you to track what has been spent by each ministry area. I favored software that allowed me to run a budget versus actual spending report every month. You should also be able to run a detailed line-item summary, which allows the staff to review charges for accuracy.

Budget Format

When putting your budget together, keep it as sim-ple as possible. This will allow those who were involved in budget discussions, such as staff and volunteers, as well as church members, to read and understand it. I prefer a budget with three or four main categories with subcategories under each. Most budgets start with an income section at the top. Under the income section, the subcategories might include general offering, investment income, building use fees, and other income. The next category might be personnel (since staff is a big expense for most churches). The subcategories under personnel might include salaries, staff insurance, staff expenses, and continuing education. The other two categories that work well for many are ministries and operations. I have also seen budgets that break out missions/outreach from ministries into its own category. The important thing is that you use labels that make sense to your church. Most accountants can help you set up a workable budget with the software to support accurate tracking of expenses.

Principles for Spending Decisions

As critical as establishing a ministry budget is, it will not serve you well without some ground rules and agreement to stated principles. For example, even though the budget has been approved, it is wise to consider limiting the amount that staff and volunteers can spend without approval. This will help you manage cash flow more effectively. Also, many churches have adopted a purchase order system. Purchase orders, for expenditures over 500 dollars, are an excellent way to manage cash while staying aware of what is being committed to. I often found myself telling the staff that money in the budget is not the same as money in the bank.

It is very important to have a policy outlining the companies from which the church will buy goods. Normally, this is not a problem for small purchases, but staff should know how to select providers for larger purchases or ongoing vendor relationships. You do not want any provider to receive, or even to appear to have received, preferential treatment when doing business with the church.

It is also wise to consider establishing spending priorities, both ministry-wide as well as within all budget categories. In the event of a downturn in donations or other income, this will make managing through those downtimes much easier and decisions more clearly understood.

I would also encourage your ministry to develop a policy to gather and maintain a cash reserve. The cash reserve should never be used for routine budget items but should be used for serious emergencies or for other unique circumstances. The board or top leadership team should approve cash reserves use. Another good practice is to accrue some money over several years for long-cycle maintenance of items such as repairing or replacing heating and air units, roofs, and carpet or flooring. Annual maintenance should be lodged in a facility line item within the operations category.

Be sure your budget is designed to serve your unique ministry. Do not use category names that do not make sense to staff or church members. Help those charged with budget adherence to participate and understand how the budget has been developed and why. Be sure it ties to your annual plan. I cannot promise everyone will be excited when you say it is time to submit a new budget, but these steps will reduce some of their anxiety. They will also increase the congregation's understanding of and confidence in the church's overall financial management, leading to greater support of the budget need.

Liability and Security Issues in Ministry
Bob R. Roberts

We live in a day and age in which lawsuits abound. Many will remember the infamous lawsuit leveled against McDonald's because a woman, in 1992, scalded herself with the hot coffee she ordered. What is even more memorable is that a jury awarded the woman 160,000 dollars in compensatory damages and 2.7 million dollars in punative damages. Approximately 20 million new civil suits are filed every year by more than one million lawyers in the United States alone. Some have suggested that lawsuits are fast becoming "the new lottery" as people file a suit to see how much they can win.

Churches often mistakenly think they are immune from litigation because their foundational purpose is to help people. After all, who would sue the do-gooders? This is a grave error; if any institution should know the liability and security issues at stake, it should be the church. It is high time for church leaders to lead their respective staffs and congregants into creating the safest environment possible in an effort to love and help people while minimizing legal risk. So where should churches begin?

Be Informed—Understand What Is at Stake

When it comes to understanding what is at stake let us consider "the big four." These are the four areas in which legal issues (whether real or alleged) most frequently occur within churches:

1. Child abuse

   This remains the single greatest legal risk for the church. Recent studies and statistics indicate that the incidence of abuse within the church is equal to that in the general population and rising. Even though it is the most significant liability issue, insurers are vague on what they will or will not cover, while some eliminate the risk, and thus the coverage, altogether.

2. Negligent supervision

   Lawsuits proving negligence most often occur when churches fail to supervise church-sponsored activities with an adequate number of qualified adults.

3. Pastoral counseling

   Counseling activities are the source of much litigation against churches every year. Unfortunately, because churches fail to take proper precautions in advance, many of the allegations are found to be true. Churches often find themselves in a "my word" versus "the other person's word" type of lawsuit.

4. Reporting abuse

   Reporting abuse is the responsibility of all church leaders. Ministers and church workers can be held legally culpable for failing to report abuse to the appropriate authorities in their area.

Obviously, the "big four" is not an exhaustive list. Other issues such as sexual harassment, defamation, and divulging confidential information can and do afflict churches. Because of the ever-changing nature of the area of liability and security, there are three individuals that the leader of a church should know well in order to further educate the church leadership: speak with your pastor to get this information.

Find out about your insurer. Take him or her out to dinner. Bring a list of questions and ask the toughest ones. Your insurer can help you know what the most crucial issues are in your area and how you can further reduce risk. Also, knowing what is and what is not covered will go a long way toward helping you train your staff and volunteers.

Have a trusted attorney. A solid attorney who stays up to date on ways to manage legal risk is a godsend. Knowing your state's laws is an absolute must, and a trusted attorney can help you stay current.

Get to know your local law enforcement. In most areas there is a specialist who deals with the kind of issues most directly related to "the big four." Invite this person to your church. Share your goals and also your fears. Discover some "best practices" she or he has observed. This person can also recommend further resources such as books and DVDs to keep your ministry informed and prepared to handle issues that present legal risks.

These three individuals can be tremendous assets in helping churches navigate uneven and awkward roads. The churches most prepared to deal with liability and security issues call upon these individuals regularly to help train church staff and volunteers.

Be Proactive—Work Diligently to Create the Safest Environment Possible

Once a church understands the issues at stake, leaders should implement policies and procedures that will most effectively limit legal risk while allowing real ministry to take place. Many lawsuits could be thwarted if church leadership made it a priority to create and maintain the safest environment possible at and around their church's facilities.

Churches should not wait for tragedy to strike before they address these issues. Churches should be sanctuaries where people can feel safe and secure. Consider that creating a safe and secure environment does not just aid ministry, it is ministry. Let us now consider five ways in which churches can be proactive to create and maintain safe and secure environments.

Provide Well-Publicized Policies and Procedures

When a church has well-publicized policies, that church can respond to negative comments by reminding the applicants that these recommendations are designed to help provide the safest possible environment for children, and that everyone who wishes to serve must go through the same process. It may also be useful to remind any naysayers that the policies are instituted to help protect them from false allegations as well.

Some examples of proactive and protective policies include not allowing minors to supervise other minors when a trained adult is not present, requiring at least two trained adults to be present at all times when supervising minors, mandating that all church employees and workers immediately report known or reasonably suspected cases of child abuse to an appointed person on the church staff, and instituting a bathroom policy that no adult should be alone in the bathroom with a child.

Having well-publicized policies and procedures will not only hinder problematic issues, but in the unfortunate event that a lawsuit is filed, the ministry that has gone the extra mile to publicize church policies will be far better protected than the church caught off guard.

Identify Various Age Groups, Leaders, and Workers

Proper identification of church leadership and appointed meeting areas goes a long way toward creating a secure environment. Consider the strategic use of things like colors, banners, signage, buttons, lanyards with tags, and identification. Identification means knowledge, and knowledge is at the heart of a secure ministry.

Identifying children is imperative especially in larger ministries. When done correctly, identifying children will help them feel part of a special group while achieving the more important purpose of safety and security.

Remember, the key to good identification is visibility; therefore, any areas in which ministry takes place should be well lit with plenty of windows and readily accessible to anyone within the church facility.

Recruit Workers

In some ministries, the only qualification needed for a person to work in the children's ministries is that the worker be breathing. The eagerness of some churches to fill ministry gaps by putting any willing, warm-bodied adult into service has often resulted in serious litigation. Smart ministries institute a waiting period of between six to twelve months before a new member may begin serving in any official capacity, and further require that workers complete an intensive training program before serving with youth and children.

Provide Forms and Documentation

Staff and volunteers should know their responsibility to write down important information at crucial times.

You should have an Incident Report Form. This form is used for events like an accident (slip and fall), fighting, and anything else out of the ordinary that could result in litigation.

Your church leadership should create a Reason to Suspect Report Form. This is the form used when an allegation of any sort is made, whether against someone within or without the church. Information that should be recorded immediately includes date, name or names of alleged perpetrator(s), persons receiving copies of the report, name or names of the victim(s), name or names of the person(s) making the allegation, and the substance of the allegation. These reports should be kept confidential and held indefinitely.

Schedule Training and Inspection

Equip your staff to build a safe and secure environment by showing them how. Strive to develop relationships in your community with experts who can help your church excel in the area of dealing with these difficult issues. Invite these experts to help train your staff and volunteers.

Make it mandatory for your staff to read through your state's legal position on child abuse.

Put your staff and volunteer policies and procedures into writing. Update them regularly and put the revision dates on the latest handouts. After you have adequately trained your staff, regularly inspect your ministry's safety and security. Be constantly honing your practices by retaining the best and refining the rest.

Be Wise—Implement Screening Policies

Every church should work to have an established process whereby all applicants for youth work, both paid staff and volunteers, are screened before serving in the church, and especially in ministries that involve youth or children. A good screening process includes the following:

1. A detailed application that any person wishing to serve in the ministry must fill out

2. Confirmation of the applicant's identity through photo ID, such as a current driver's license or passport

3. References, especially past ministries in which the applicant has served. Keep detailed records along with the applicant's original application in one file.

4. An official background check

Official background checks are nonnegotiable. If your ministry has not implemented this yet, begin immediately. Start by running thorough background checks on anyone eighteen years of age and older who is currently serving in the church, especially with youth. Background checks should be performed for both paid staff and volunteers. Contact your local law enforcement for details on how to begin systematic background checks.

The church should make clear to all applicants the purpose for the screening, and assure them that all information will be treated as strictly confidential.

Be Ready—Know How to Respond Before It Happens

Studies show that child abuse is happening in the United States at the alarming rate of one incidence every fifteen seconds. When an incident occurs, it is the church's responsibility to respond quickly and in accordance with the law.

When an incident happens, the ministry should immediately respond with concern and empathy, making any applicable resources (such as counseling) available during the situation.

Consider these following five questions:

1. How will your ministry respond to allegations?

2. How will your ministry respond to media attention?

3. What practices are currently in place in your ministry that help minimize legal risk?

4. What practices need to be put in place in your ministry that will help create a safer, more secure environment?

5. Is there currently anyone serving in ministries that involve children or youth that raise some "red flags" in your mind? If so, why?

Remember, a church should protect children from harm. A church should protect workers that volunteer their time from false accusations and compromised testimonies. A church should be a good steward of all that the Lord has given it and take necessary steps to protect the ministry from financial liability, perversion of power, and spiritual damage (Prov. 22:1). May we endeavor to glorify God by creating environments within our churches worthy of His character.

Part Five
Problem Solving

A Biblical Perspective on Problems

Wally Weaver

The congregation had prayed and looked forward to this moment for nearly two years. Unfortunately, anticipation, enthusiasm, and excitement for hearing their new pastor quickly turned to shock and disbelief. Rather than the expected order of service, a church official stepped to the pulpit and informed the congregation they were victims of a fraudulent scheme. As details unfolded, many became angry, hurt, and disillusioned. Some members yelled at one another, made unfounded accusations, and even used Scripture to harm one another. While a few people left in disgust, the majority just sat there, numb and speechless, hoping someone would make sense of all they had just witnessed. It was in this setting that the church's new pastor walked toward the pulpit for the first time. A hush came over the sanctuary and every eye was focused upon him, anxiously waiting to see how he would respond.

If you were in this pastor's shoes, what would you do? What thoughts might be running through your head? What could you say to this hurting congregation?

What most would describe as a horrible beginning actually became a defining moment for this church and its pastor. In the span of an hour, a congregation had gone from anticipation and excitement to anger, chaos, and despair and ended in personal repentance, reconciliation, and restored fellowship. Far from being a potentially devastating blow to this body and its future ministry, the events of that evening became the very thing that God used to unify the church and establish the credibility of their new pastor. Fortunately, most leaders will never have to experience what this pastor went through on his first night in the pulpit. Even so, every church leader must prepare beforehand if he is to provide godly leadership when it is needed most.

The Big Picture

Perspective is everything when it comes to managing difficulties and leading others. What people believe about God, themselves, the church, and other people has a profound impact on the way they perceive the world and interact with others. As a church leader you have tremendous opportunity to influence others with a biblical worldview. Your preaching, teaching, and personal lifestyle can help others understand the Bible and learn how to apply it to their daily lives.

There is an old Chinese proverb that says "The best time to plant a tree was twenty years ago. The second best time is now." The same is true for preparing for the uncertainties of life. If you have not already had opportunity to do so, today is the perfect time to evaluate your approach to problem solving in light of the Scriptures.

Let us begin by defining the word *problem*. Generally speaking, most people perceive hindrances or obstacles to a predetermined plan or goal as problems. Anyone or anything that gets in the way of "the plan" or achieving "the goal" is seen as a problem. Surprisingly, although the world may seem plagued by problems today, the word *problem* is rarely used in Scripture.[6] What some call problems, the Bible refers to as burdens, trials, and tribulation. Jesus and the apostle James clearly taught that all these things are part of the normal Christian life, yet many people today believe that obedience to God should be equated with a life relatively free of hardship and full of blessing (John 16:33; Heb. 11; James 1:2–4). Most of the people God has used in significant ways throughout history, however, have suffered greatly as a consequence of their obedience to God (Luke 9:23; Heb. 11). Many of these same individuals even died before they saw the fulfillment of God's promise, yet their faith never wavered. It is in the midst of these hardships and human impossibilities that God is glorified and Christians experience His power and faithfulness.

How Big Is Your God?

When the whole Israelite army stood paralyzed in fear of a problem named Goliath, it took a little shepherd boy with a strong faith in a sovereign God to confront the Philistine giant and boldly declare, "This day will the LORD deliver thee into mine hand" (1 Sam. 17:46). The Israelites were so focused on Goliath they had lost all perspective of God's greatness and involvement in their lives. Our giants today come in many different forms, yet God's faithfulness has not changed. He is still our

Strong Tower and Deliverer (2 Sam. 22:2; Ps. 18:2; 32:7; 61:3; 144:2; Prov. 18:10). Unfortunately, like the Israelites, we can become paralyzed with fear and anxiety when distracted by life's troubles. The more we focus on problems, the bigger they become and the more distant God seems. Are you facing any giants today? If so, ask God to show what they look like through His eyes. It is all about perspective—bringing our understanding of situations and circumstances into agreement with God's.

Church leaders must be unwavering in their pursuit of God's wisdom and guidance. The counsel of the Lord and the truths of Scripture are the filters through which all decisions must pass. To neglect or minimize the importance of this step in your problem solving is a tragic mistake and opens oneself to the influence of our enemy (Ps. 33:3–22; 119; Prov. 19:21; Isa. 30:1; 2 Cor. 10:3–6; James 3:13–18).

You Are Not Alone

Few things in life can be lonelier than serving as a leader in a local church. Most church members look to the leaders as their shepherds, counselors, and examples of what a Christian should be like. Unfortunately, the high expectations and respect that congregants have for their church leaders often make it difficult for leaders to develop close relationships within the local body. Even so, leaders cannot afford to ignore the counsel of others when it comes to problem solving and other important leadership decisions affecting the church.

Scripture reminds church leaders of the importance of godly counsel from other people as a secondary means to clarify and affirm the Lord's intentions and to protect the church from bad decisions (Prov. 11:14; 15:22). Since pride, control issues, and personal agendas are most likely to emerge when others' input is being considered, church leaders need to exercise discernment throughout the process (Matt. 7:15–20; Acts 20:28–31; 1 Tim. 4:1-5). The Jerusalem Council is a great example of how the early church dealt constructively with concerns related to faith and practice (Acts 15:1–36).

Despite our best efforts, even mature Christians will sometimes disagree. The disagreement that Paul and Barnabas had over John Mark is a good example of how God can take something that outwardly looks bad and use it for His greater good (Acts 15:37–41). Their failure to agree regarding John Mark's involvement led to two missionary trips instead of one. What looked like unwillingness to compromise or work together was used providentially for a greater expansion of the church. Are you dealing with situations that have reached an impasse? If so, have you considered the possibility that God may want you to pursue more than one solution at the same time? It may be that God desires to do an even greater work than anyone envisions (Eph. 3:20).

Putting It All Together

While it would be inappropriate to suggest that there is a "one-size-fits-all" approach to a biblical perspective on problem solving, Scripture does provide many insights:

1. Everything begins and ends with God (Ps. 90:2; Acts 17:24–25; Col. 1:15–23; Rev. 1:8; 4:11).

2. Do not allow distractions to redirect your focus (Heb. 12:1–2).

3. God has a plan (Pss. 37:18–31; 139:13–16; Isa. 46:8–13; Eph. 2:10).

4. God is in control, regardless of how things may seem (Prov. 16:1–3, 9; Rom. 8:18–39).

5. Pray (Eph. 3:14–21; Col. 1:9–14; 1 Thess. 5:16–18; 1 Tim. 2:1–4; James 1:5–7).

6. Do not develop plans or a response until you have heard from the Lord.

7. Look at the bigger picture—is God doing something that you have never seen before or did not anticipate?

8. Wait on God (Pss. 46:10; 127:1).

9. Guard your heart (Prov. 4:23).

10. Address any pride or control issues (Prov. 16:5; 29:23; James 4:6–10; 1 Peter 5:5–7).

11. Be flexible (Prov. 16:9).

12. Resolve anger quickly (Prov. 15:1; Eph. 4:25–32; James 1:19–20).

13. Avoid worldly solutions (Ps. 1; Prov. 3:5–7; Isa. 55:8–9; 1 Cor. 1:18–31; James 3:13–18; 4:1–5).

14. Do your homework (Neh. 2:11–20; Prov. 18:13, 17): What are the needs? What resources are available? What is the history? How did things get this way in the first place?

15. Involve others.

16. Share the vision (Prov. 29:18).

17. Pay attention to what others are saying.

18. Seek godly counsel.

19. Listen to your critics—there is usually an element of truth in what they are saying.

20. Utilize the giftedness of those around you (Rom. 12:1–8; 1 Cor. 12; Eph 4:7–16; 1 Peter 4:10–11).

21. Delegate whenever possible.

22. Have realistic expectations.

23. Anticipate opposition from others (Neh. 2:9, 19; 4:1–3, 7–9; John 10:10; Acts 20:28–31; 1 Peter 5:8–11).

24. Counter trials and tribulation (John 16:33; 1 Peter 4:12–19).

25. Rely upon God for strength and support (2 Chron. 16:9; Isa. 40:28–31; 41:10–13; Phil. 4:13).

26. Do not limit God (Matt. 19:26; Luke 1:37; Eph. 3:20–21).

27. Demonstrate love in all things (John 13:34–35; 1 Cor. 13; 1 John 4:7–21).

Encountering problems is an inevitable part of life, and often beyond our control. Yet church leaders have a unique opportunity to influence the way others understand and respond to life's challenges.

> If there be therefore any consolation in Christ, if any comfort of love, if any fellowship of the Spirit, if any bowels and mercies, Fulfil ye my joy, that ye be likeminded, having the same love, being of one accord, of one mind. Let nothing be done through strife or vainglory; but in lowliness of mind let each esteem other better than themselves. Look not every man on his own things, but every man also on the things of others. (Phil. 2:1–4)

Damage Control
and Prevention
Ron Kairdolf

"I love God; it's the church I can't stand."

How many times have you heard this statement? It is said by those who have been wounded by the church and by those outside looking in. Something has gone terribly wrong in the church world. Let us face it, some churches make nice people mean, happy people sad, and creative people miserable. As a result, unchurched people stay away in droves, church members become church hoppers, and pastors are dropping out of ministry at an alarming rate. Rather than providing a healthy environment of loving reconciliation, the church is often perceived as an agent of alienation.

It does not have to be this way.

In fact, the marks of a healthy church are changed lives, restored families, faithful friendships, and a vibrant and positive faith growing in its members. That should be the goal of any committed church leader.

But that goal cannot be reached without the recognition that a church is made up of imperfect people. And where imperfect people gather regularly, problems and conflict are inevitable. In fact, it is impossible to have a healthy church without conflict. Have you ever realized that two-thirds of the New Testament was written to churches experiencing conflict?

For most ministry leaders the word *conflict* is a nasty one and something to be avoided at all costs. Though no one enjoys confrontation, we must learn to embrace it. As a church planter, I have come to realize that how you manage conflict will often determine the health and growth of your church.

One dazed pastor lamented, "How can things seem to be going so good and fall apart in an instant?" The problems encountered and the ensuing discord may look different in every church, but I can assure you, every stage of growth brings with it a potential for conflict. A healthy church is a growing church. Growth brings change and change creates conflict. Conflict handled correctly enables a leader and the congregation to experience a healthy body life and a dynamic walk of faith.

Four Stages of Growth and Conflict Resolution

Stage One: Laying the Foundation

"If the foundations be destroyed, what can the righteous do?" (Ps. 11:3).

You do not have to be a structural engineer to understand how important the foundation is to the strength and integrity of a building. Just so, every successful leader realizes how vital a solid foundation is for the implementation of vision and successful strategy of a church.

One of the most dangerous forms of conflict in a church body is theological debate. Creating an environment wherein truth is presented in a simple,

straightforward, and consistent way will serve to eliminate doctrinal conflict to a large degree. Regardless of
your church affiliation, certain New Testament doctrines
and principals are universally foundational. Teaching
the biblical truth about Christ is vital to the health of
any church. It is paramount that church leadership holds
fast to the basic tenets of Christianity and communicates them with joy, honesty, and clarity. We must strive
to avoid meaningless arguments on the nonessentials.
Make it your aim to concentrate on the majors.

It is also very important that your entire leadership
team be in agreement with the pastor's teaching, by living
as examples. This can best be accomplished by putting
into place "functional guidelines"—attributes essential
to the furtherance of the gospel and the outworking
of your vision. For my church, the list is quite uncom-
plicated: simplicity, sincerity, and sacrifice. One of my
mentors taught me early in my ministry the importance
and power of this short list of functional guidelines.
From that time, I have adopted these attributes as a style
of leadership for my ministry and our leadership team.

If your method of ministry is complicated and confusing, you are headed for conflict. The message of the
gospel is simple, straightforward, deep, and honest. Your
ministry should be the same. If your leadership style
comes across as being superficial and fake, conflict and
discord will follow in your wake.

I encourage you, wherever you are as a church
leader, to go back and reexamine your foundation. Do
you know what you believe and why? Are your beliefs

firmly grounded on the Word of God? Have you clearly communicated your beliefs to your church? What are your own "functional guidelines" for ministry? Have you defined and developed a healthy Christlike leadership style?

Stage Two: Establishing a Leadership Team

One way to create potentially damaging conflict is in how you select and empower a leadership team. If the staff, department heads, and servant leaders are not willing to live a sacrificial life for the sheep, your congregation is heading toward strife, discord, and conflict. A leadership team is an extension of the pastoral ministry. If leaders represent the pastor well, growth will result. If they act or live in a way that contradicts who the pastor is or what he teaches, they will cause damage that could take years to recover from.

Develop and Recruit Leaders—Be Careful with Volunteers. Volunteers are generally well-meaning Christians looking for an opportunity to be used. However, be very careful before you release them into leadership, by trying to isolate their motivation for ministry and determining their maturity in Christ. The wrong person in the wrong position can drive a pastor to the point of distraction and may even sap the energy and joy from the church as a whole.

Below is a list of seven volunteers who are not ready to serve on your leadership team. Love them, train them, do not quit on them; but please do not give them any kind of leadership position in the church until they have matured and put aside these childish behaviors:

The Nega-Saints. These people are easy to spot. They have a negative attitude toward just about everything and it is almost always contagious. They are prone to say things like "It's too expensive," "the music is too loud," or "we've tried that before and it didn't work." A negative attitude wars against faith and frustrates your servant leaders.

The Networker. This person is just the opposite of the Nega-Saint. In fact, this person wants to meet every person she or he can. These folks come across as being enthusiastic and encouraging. However, they see everyone as a potential customer for their vitamins, juicers, diet plans, and so on.

The Bible Thumper. These people are amateur theologians and usually have a passion for a certain theological position. Because of their knowledge of the Word they look like a great asset to the ministry. However, people will soon tire of their theological agenda.

The Insult Artist. These are gifted people who know how to criticize you and everyone else without being caught. You often walk away asking yourself, "Did he say what I thought he said?" If you confront this person, he or she will be appalled that you took him or her the "wrong way" or will state that he or she was "only joking." Be careful with the "insult artist."

The Steno Typist. Like court reporters, these are the people who keep record of everything other leaders say that they consider unspiritual. They have an incredible memory and have a way of understanding and repeating things out of context.

The Money Person. Every church will have to deal with one of these folks from time to time. Do not take the bait. If you give in to a wealthy person who uses his or her giving as a means of approving or disapproving of your ministry, you ministry is heading toward a major meltdown. You are better off cutting the budget than giving in to the agenda of the "money person."

The Busybody. These are the people who meddle into other people's business. The popularity of on-line social networking has given these folks a new way to monitor other church members' activities and comments. Busybodies on Facebook and other sites are fast becoming a headache to many leaders. I personally recommend that every leader open a Facebook account and make his presence known. If for no other reason, your presence and interaction will add some level of accountability.

As you recruit leaders and servants, look to the apostle Paul as an example of one raised up by God as a leader. Paul's apostolic calling was revealed to him only three days after his encounter on the road to Damascus (Acts 9:15). Even though Paul had a personal visitation from Christ, he did not promote himself. He was willing to be taught, tested, and matured over a period of years. Finally, at the right time, Paul was sent out by the elders in Antioch into his apostolic ministry. From his own experience, Paul wrote these instructions for potential leaders: "And let these also first be proved; then let them use the office of a deacon, being found blameless" (1 Tim. 3:10).

Stage Three: Defining Direction

A healthy church body must share a vision—a common journey and destination. Growth cannot happen and a church cannot experience healthy body life without direction and purpose. It is a leader's duty to acquire direction from the Lord and to communicate that vision to the ones he serves. Your ability to answer and articulate the answers to the following questions will determine your level of success in stage three.

I cannot overemphasize the importance of a clear word from God in determining the direction of your ministry. Do not take the easy road of simply adopting the vision of another church. Do the work yourself. Invest the time in prayer and fasting. God will give you a specific vision distinctly for your ministry.

In determining God's call on your own church body, be careful that you do not become a "niche church"—a ministry that is so focused on one aspect of the kingdom that it becomes unbalanced. It is my belief that an authentic kingdom-minded church will desire to minister to the whole community with the whole gospel.

Finally, watch out for people who have their own agenda. Often well-meaning people see an opportunity to capitalize on the growth of the church. They may be looking for a platform, financial aid, or a staff position. Keep the vision true and do not let people distract you.

One more thing: communicate, communicate, communicate. Use every available media outlet to keep the vision in front of the church. Web sites, Facebook, Twitter, videos, and e-mails can all be used to cast the vision and define your direction. Keep it fresh, keep it alive, and celebrate your accomplishments.

Stage Four: Giving Ministry Away

There is a need inside every believer to be corrected, trained, and released into ministry. We are a body and every member matters. As Paul says in 1 Corinthians 12:22, "Much more those members of the body, which seem to be more feeble, are necessary." People denied the ability to operate in God-given gifts and talents become frustrated, disillusioned, and defeated. They often make a career of church hopping or may even fall away entirely.

It is the job of church leaders to equip (Eph. 4:11–12) and release church members into ministry. Many churches never grow into this stage of ministry because of fear. Releasing members into ministry requires pastors to allow delegated leaders to serve within the context of the vision without asking permission for their every move. It is at this stage in church growth that the potential for damaging conflict reaches its highest point. That is a frightening path for pastors with control issues, but it is the only course that leads to health and vitality in the local church. The fruitfulness of a church body begins to multiply as people are released into their giftedness. Confidence increases, visions are realized, and the kingdom comes into clear and exciting focus.

Epilogue

Simplicity, sincerity, and sacrifice—when these are present in a ministry lives are changed, beginning with the leadership and "trickling down" to the congregation. As it was in the early church, it will again be: the world will be attracted to Christ by the love and power existing in His church. And those who are members of His body will be enabled to walk into the destiny prepared for them by the hand of Almighty God. What joy it would be at the end of our ministry to echo Jesus' words, "those that thou gavest me I have kept, and none of them is lost" (John 17:12). Lord, let it be so.

Dealing with Difficult Members

Monty Waldron

The essence of ministry is expressed in the Great Commission Jesus gave to His disciples prior to His ascension. "Go ye therefore, and teach all nations, baptizing them in the name of the Father, and of the Son, and of the Holy Ghost: Teaching them to observe all things whatsoever I have commanded you" (Matt. 28:19–20). At face value, this envisions leading unbelievers into a trusting relationship with Jesus Christ and then guiding them into a growing relationship with God. Nothing, it seems, could be more fulfilling and enjoyable than participating in this beautiful work of spiritual formation. But if you have engaged in discipleship for any length of time, you know it can be painfully difficult, especially when dealing with difficult members of Christ's body. By difficult, I mean resistant.

Having said that, we should acknowledge that all of us are resistant, to varying degrees, at different points of our walk with God. It is the nature of our flesh to oppose the work of the Spirit (Gal. 5:17). The residue of sin in us, though it has been rendered powerless at the time of our conversion, is like the deep roots of a fallen tree. Unearthing those roots is far more challenging than cutting away what is above the surface. Discipleship is a lifelong process of uprooting the deeply ingrained deeds of the flesh while cultivating the fruit of the Spirit. The willingness of the disciple plays a major role in the progress of both. I am addressing how we might approach discipleship in the life of a believer who resists the transformational work of sanctification, initiated by the Spirit and cultivated by the community of faith. I am personally encouraged by the fact that the majority of our New Testament letters were prompted by the need to correct people in the church who could have been considered "difficult members."

Lead with Humility

As leaders, it is imperative that we approach our calling to spiritual oversight with great humility. I understand this to mean that we should not think more highly of ourselves (or more lowly) than we ought to (Rom. 12:3). We should recognize that we are no less capable of sin than those we are serving. The moment we view ourselves as an exception to temptation, we expose ourselves to the deception of pride and to the probability of a fall. Scripture urges us to keep watch on ourselves (Gal. 6:1) and to guard our heart with all vigilance (Prov. 4:23). The more dependent we are upon God for our own walk of faith, the more able we will be to effectively engage the lives of those who are yet unwilling to walk in unity with the body of Christ. And that is just what we are called to do as spiritual leaders. Paul charged Timothy to "preach the word; be instant in season, out of season; reprove, rebuke, exhort with all long suffering and doctrine" (2 Tim. 4:2). Elsewhere he urged brothers in the church of Thessalonica to "warn them that are unruly, comfort the feebleminded, support the weak, be patient toward all men" (1 Thess. 5:14). While this can be awkward and unpleasant, it is the work of discipleship to which we are called.

Addressing issues with a difficult member is a delicate matter for sure. How, when, and what we communicate is vitally important. Poorly chosen and poorly timed words can be devastating. I am not trying to be overly dramatic. I am simply trying to convey the immense power of the words we use, particularly in confrontational situations. We read, "Death and life are in the power of the tongue: and they that love it shall eat the fruit thereof" (Prov. 18:21). Elsewhere it says that there is more hope for a fool than for a person who is hasty in his words (Prov. 29:20). We would be wise to prayerfully frame our thoughts before expressing them to persons in need of correction. The last thing we want to do is create needless obstacles to our intended message simply out of poor preparation.

Have the Proper Motivation

We should also keep in mind that careless communication is more than unwise, it is also unloving. Love is always to be our primary motive as we relate to one another, which means our message should have as its aim the greater good of the one receiving it. I can easily become consumed with what I want to say rather than what others may need to hear and how they need to hear it—all the more reason to be very attentive to the Holy Spirit throughout our communication. Paul's words to Timothy are apt in this regard: "Now the end of the commandment is charity out of a pure heart, and of a good conscience, and of faith unfeigned" (1 Tim. 1:5). That purpose is applicable to speakers and hearers alike.

Avoid Common Pitfalls

I have found a few practical things to have been helpful over the years when I have engaged difficult members. When I have failed to practice these disciplines, I have experienced serious setbacks. First of all, impersonal communication is rarely, if ever, effective. We live in an age where e-mail, text messages, social networking, and other detached forms of communication are common. But using these outlets has often proved to make matters worse rather than better. Electronic messages are very easily misunderstood and misinterpreted. They lack vital clarifying features like tone of voice, facial expression, and the opportunity for immediate dialogue. All the reader has to go on is the written word, which can often leave much to the imagination. Recipients of written messages are left to guess about their meaning and intentions. I have also found that we tend to be less sensitive when typing on a computer than we are face-to-face. Finally, electronic conversations seem to escalate easily and take on a hostile life of their own. It is well worth the time and energy to arrange for face-to-face conversations.

Another trap to avoid is the passive path of triangulation. Rather than going straight to the person needing to be addressed, it seems easier to have conversations with third parties who honestly have no reason to be in the loop. It is imperative that we, as leaders, avoid this. But I have found that I am often more on the receiving end of this than on the giving end, especially with difficult members. They will contact me with a complaint about a member in their small group or another member of our staff (youth pastors are frequently approached this way by parents in an attempt to address issues with their children). When this happens, I respond by asking if they have talked directly to the person they have mentioned. If not, then I will ask them to start with that person before involving me in the conversation. I am glad to assist if two parties are at an impasse, but our folks need to strive to settle issues themselves first before involving others.

Ask Questions

Another helpful practice when dealing with difficult members is to live in the world of facts. Assumptions are relational killers, and controversy is usually chock-full of them. In a confrontational situation I am resolved to steer the conversation away from what might be to what is. When something is unknown or potentially misunderstood, the best approach is to believe the best and investigate what is unknown. If there is a legitimate issue, it is more likely to come to light as a result of good questions. One of the most important things I do with difficult members is ask a lot of questions. By doing that, I am modeling the very thing I would like for them to do, and graciously exposing those ways in which they are clouding the issues with their own unfounded ideas. Please note that this is not an interrogation, but a genuine inquiry intended to surface known facts about the matter at hand.

If Necessary, Exercise Church Discipline

At the end of the day, all of the best practices may not break through the hard heart of a stubborn or divisive member. In that case, leaders are wise to develop core convictions around the process of church discipline. First and foremost, church discipline must be exercised with the goal of restoration. Like a good shepherd, the goal is to gently but intentionally bring estranged sheep back into the fold. Matthew 18 outlines a well-defined process that allows a difficult member multiple opportunities to reestablish unity with the body. It is worth mentioning again our need as leaders to initiate this process from a posture of humility.

When I am prompted to do so, I clearly communicate with the member being disciplined when that process has become necessary and what steps need to be taken in order to repair broken relationships. This begins with an individual conversation and expands to wider circles of involvement when the member is unresponsive. I clarify that the actions of leadership are not punitive but restorative in nature. I also explain that eventual separation in the case of resistance is their choice, not ours. Finally, members who reject our attempts at restoration are told that the door remains open should they decide they want to reconcile and address the issues that prompted disciplinary action. As a pastor, I have embraced the idea that maturity is ultimately more important than membership. And it may be that separation will be the very thing God will use to bring about the maturity He longs to produce in someone's life. I am grateful to those who loved me enough to confront sin in my life and wholeheartedly affirm the truth "faithful are the wounds of a friend" (Prov. 27:6).

Removing Ineffective Leaders Without Losing Them
Dr. Craig A. Green

A God-ordained church leader can feel like he is herding cats if other members of a leadership team are either asleep on the job or worse: actively turning sheep into cats. Whether intentional or not, ineffective leadership can make the already difficult task of spiritual leadership become a nearly impossible job, not unlike cat herding.

Every leader in your church is by default a pastor. We all know that pastors are shepherds who lead, not ranchers who herd. All leaders hope their beloved flock consists of compliant sheep, not wild and frenzied cats. A couple decades as a pastor has taught me, however, that in the real world sheep bite, shepherds are oftentimes tempted to herd, and leaders—elders, deacons, or whatever you call them—can stir up or tear up the flock so badly that a pastor-leader's job can … well … stink like a litter box.

While I strongly urge you to not compare your flock to cats, I also empathize with you on those days when you wonder if cat ranching would not be easier than trying to shepherd a flock of people. It is difficult to put into words the depth of anguish felt by those of us who pour our hearts out in genuine service, with sensitivity to the Lord and His Spirit, all the while longing for the next chapter in Acts to be written about our congregation, only to be stifled, fought, badgered, ignored, and ridiculed for the effort. Many problems can stem from a pastor and church leaders moving in an opposite direction, or just not moving at all.

Ineffective leaders can turn flocks into herds and sheep into cats. Ineffective leaders can stifle progress and stir up dissension. Ineffective leaders can confuse and compromise even the most godly of visions and plans. In consultation with your pastor, ineffective leaders need to be removed from leadership. As a leader yourself, however, you want this to be done in a way that allows the other person to remain part of the flock. You desire for them to feel loved and affirmed even after their season in leadership has passed. You want to remain friends with them, dreading the confrontation and possibility of conflict that may come from removing them from leadership.

As a fellow disciple of Jesus Christ, you passionately love co-laboring leaders, even those who are or have become ineffective. However, keep this in mind: while biting sheep will be with us until the end of the age, ineffective leaders will only be with us as long as pastor-leaders fail to address the issue. By confronting ineffective leadership, you may well reduce the frequency of sheep attacks. More important, you may well be used by God to bring healing and restoration to a brother or sister who is, in all likelihood, as frustrated about the situation as you are.

Oftentimes, ineffective leaders have simply grown weary of doing good and need a break. Some may have bought into God's vision for the body fifteen or twenty years ago, but find it hard to invest in what He is envisioning for today. Still others may be in a position of leadership simply because of their worldly successes. Oftentimes, congregations promote bankers, doctors, accountants, and businessmen to leadership positions, confusing the talents used in the workplace for the gifts of the Holy Spirit necessary for effective spiritual leadership. Regardless of the reasons for a person's ineffectiveness in leadership, it is imperative that your pastor guide you and your fellow leaders so that you, in turn, will partner with your pastor in effectively leading the church. This only happens when leaders are submitted together to the Great Shepherd, Jesus.

Here are some suggestions on how to go about removing ineffective leaders while, one hopes, remaining their friend, and co-laborer:

1. Know the polity (governmental structure) of your congregation.

   In many situations, leaders rotate in and out of leadership positions as prescribed by local bylaws, denominational rules, or traditions. The answer to your frustration may only be a few months away. Many congregations, however, need to resubmit themselves to the governmental structures of their tradition in order for the system to actually work. Smaller congregations, especially, tend to put the same people on the same committees year after year. Allow the polity of the tradition your congregation is associated with do what it was designed to do. If you pastor a congregation that lacks a structure for leadership rotation, consider the value of implementing it. Remember, however, that there is a downside—great leaders also rotate in and out in this system, just like the marginal ones.

2. Give the leader a choice.

Quite often the leader is just as frustrated as you are. He may well be glad to remove himself from leadership if he can do so without feeling used or abused. While it is not our job to protect others' ego or pride, it is also not our job to destroy their sense of self-worth. Lovingly discuss the situation and give the leader a choice to step down, step into another ministry, take some time off, or whatever he may choose. Allow him to own his decision and to shape, at least in part, the conversations surrounding his decision. You will go a long way in affirming and loving a Blood-bought brother or sister if you will just give him or her some choices.

3. Confront, but never play politics.

Confrontation does not come easy for most of us. Unfortunately, using techniques such as manipulation, domination, and intimidation often does. Do not give in to the political control methods, however. Playing political games in the church is a slap in the face of the One who refuses to play along: Jesus. Sooner or later, controlling others through the use of political strategies will destroy both the congregation and the ministry of the game-player. Ineffective leaders do not need to be tricked, pushed, or scared out of their positions. They need to be lovingly confronted, however, to help them recognize options, as well as shortcomings. Confrontation need not be loud and angry, and usually will not be, as long as the truth is spoken in love.

4. Separate the frustration of failed leadership from the joy of mutual ministry.

   The leader who is driving you nuts is also a Blood-bought, Jesus-loving, Spirit-filled companion in Christ. Take the time to pray through the frustration until you can honestly and lovingly forgive, embrace, and share the joy of the Lord with that person. Before you confront a person, make sure all bitterness and frustration have given way to joy and peace. Separating the frustrations of positional failure from the recognition of personal value is essential. Even when hatefully treated, Christians simply do not have the "right" to hang on to a grudge.

5. Remember that John Mark was once an "ineffective leader" (Acts 15:35–40).

For 2,000 years theologians have wondered what set the stage for John Mark's restoration and maturation as a leader. Was it Paul's stern confrontation, or Barnabas's gentle encouragement, that made the difference? Barnabas was right: taking a failed leader under your wing with acceptance, forgiveness, and encouragement can powerfully allow the healing needed for that person to become a great leader. Paul was right: confronting a serious failure of character with boldness and prophetic insight can cause a person to face his fears and weaknesses and powerfully allow the healing needed for that person to become a great leader. Perhaps it took both confrontation and encouragement—both a Paul and a Barnabas—to complete the good work God had begun in John Mark. Regardless, he stayed in the church and became a great leader, which should bring hope to us all. Finally, remember that both Paul and Barnabas were great leaders, and yet their disagreement became so heated that they parted ways—and God used the division to bring multiplication. Sometimes great leaders will disagree. Sometimes leadership teams will split apart. Sometimes people leave. As long as

> prayer in the Holy Spirit is involved, however, God will eventually bring good out of it all.

No one said that being a leader would be easy, and some of the hardest times you will ever know will involve struggles with failed and ineffective leaders. While these suggestions should help, the truth is that there will almost certainly be conflict, disagreement, rumors, and pain associated with leadership changes. Sooner or later, someone you love will leave. Sooner rather than later, someone will call for your removal. Do not allow yourself to become an ineffective leader in the midst of it all. Lead. Pray fervently. Shepherd the flock. Love passionately and cry occasionally. Forgive freely and battle bitterness every step of the way.

Integrating New People into Existing Groups
Kurt Jenkins

Lost in the Airport

If you have ever been in an airport, you know the excitement that previously filled your mind about flying is quickly replaced by an anxiety that seems to paralyze your smallest decisions. Going on your dream vacation that once brought thoughts of relaxation and fun are now overshadowed by the stress of checking your bags, making it through the x-ray scanner, finding the correct terminal, and making it to your gate on time. Flying for the first time has caused enough strife in some people's lives that they have vowed to never fly again.

The same holds true for hundreds of visitors who pass through the doors of your church each year. The excitement of trying a new congregation can easily be overshadowed by feelings of anxiety. Visitors may fear being embarrassed or put in an uncomfortable situation. They may not know where the nursery or guest center is, or what the correct procedure is for accessing either one.

However, if the local body welcomes them and makes them feel accepted on a Sunday morning, the task is still large to actually get them integrated into well-established groups that exist within the church. If they get lost while trying to find their way, they may never travel this way again.

Fortunately, there are tools for churches that help integrate visitors until they are fully committed members who are growing and serving.

The Overall Purpose

The overall purpose of an airport is to successfully get you to your destination as quickly and easily as possible, with little or no delays or cancellations. It provides the means of transportation, but you have the choice of when and where to fly. An airport can therefore be looked at as a releasing agency.

Is the church's purpose the same as an airport? Are we called to be a releasing agency for new people who come into our fellowship? The Great Commission, as well as Jesus' words to the disciples in Acts 1, makes it pretty clear that we are to release our people into kingdom work, not control their destination with rules, delays, and inconveniences.

- Matthew 28:19: Go ye therefore, and teach all nations.
- Acts 1:8: Ye shall receive power, after that the Holy Ghost is come upon you: and ye shall be witnesses unto me both in Jerusalem, and in all Judaea, and in Samaria, and unto the uttermost part of the earth.

Jesus did not have a ministry of controlling others with flight regulations and bag fees. He did not have a limited view of what someone could become in Christ, or what he or she could accomplish in His power. He was a master at releasing people into their destinies through freedom from sin.

We must admit that we sometimes have preconceived notions about new people. In our minds we already have them placed into the group or ministry that we think is best for them without ever getting to know what God is already accomplishing in them. However, when we assume the role of being a sending agency, our purpose goes from what we think is best to what He thinks is best. One hopes that the purpose of releasing new people to the destination that God has planned for them will help us build an effective process of integration.

A Clear Process

Fortunately for me, the closest major airport I travel with is clearly marked from the time you enter the baggage check-in to the time you get to your gate. The employees are kind, the process is simple, and my anxiety is minimal. I feel confident that I am going to pass through each stage of their process smoothly without being embarrassed, getting lost, or being late for my flight. It sets up my entire trip for success.

Our church also tries to make the process clear for people looking to get integrated. We use three simple words to define our mission: *connect, grow, serve* (connect with God and connect others to God; grow individually and in a small group; serve in ministry and mission). Each word highlights one aspect of our discipleship process, which newcomers learn more about in our easy entry point called the "Connection Series." Our Connection Series is a four-week interactive course that introduces newcomers to our mission, vision, and core values, while providing them with clear next steps. As people complete our Connection Series, they are confident in the direction they are traveling and are introduced to those who can help guide them along the way.

Church leaders should seriously consider developing a clear entry point for all newcomers to your church. This is the first step of getting new people integrated into all other aspects of the church beyond Sunday morning. In our course, we discuss very practical ways people can connect with others, grow in their faith, and serve in a ministry. Your course should give a big picture overview of the beliefs and core values of your church, along with how Sunday school or small groups are structured. This entry point should also give practical tools that help identify how God has formed them for serving in ministry. The more they learn about themselves during this process, the easier the integration will be.

We limit our Connection Series to four weeks, taking into consideration that these individuals may not yet want to attend an eight- or twelve-week course. We also keep it as conversational as possible so they begin to form friendships within that group. We have seen couples and individuals join established groups together so they already have familiar faces during the transition. We also have several of our pastors or other leaders lead each of these discussions so newcomers have more than just the senior pastor as a contact person. This helps spread the responsibility of integration and strengthens our practice of Ephesians 4:11–12 ministry, where the pastors are not expected to do all the work, but rather to equip and release others to do the work of the ministry.

Ministry Recommendation Form

Name:		Date:

Age:	Attends Which Service:	
Marital Status:	Length at Church:	
Children:	Former Church:	
Number of Years a Christian:	Water Baptism: Yes/No	

Current Vocation:	Likes Most:	Likes Least:

Additional Education/Training:

Bible Reading: Daily/Weekly/Sporadically	Prayer: Daily/Weekly/Sporadically	Fasting: Weekly/Monthly/Sporadically

Personality Type:	Notes:		

Gifts: 1)	2)	3)	4)

Leadership Style: Notes:
Pioneer/Strategic/Administrative/
Team/Pastoral/Encouraging

Skills: 1)	2)	3)
Passions: 1)	2)	3)
Works Well with These People Groups: 1)		2)

Past Ministry Experience:

Past Painful Experiences:

Current Struggles:

Current Ministries:

Availability: Weekly/Monthly/As Needed

Additional Comments:

Recommendations from Pastoral Team: (include follow-up pastor)

1)

2)

3)

The X-Ray Scanner

The most uncomfortable process in an airport is going through the x-ray scanner. There is something unnerving about a complete stranger looking "beyond" my clothes as I simultaneously obey his or her commands to put all my valuables in a tray that I lose sight of for several seconds.

I guess you can say we complete an "x-ray scan" on each newcomer who attends our Connection Series. Each attendee is given instructions on how to complete various inventories that help reveal different aspects of their unique ministry design. We use an excellent online resource that helps identify a person's strengths in the areas of personality, spiritual gifts, leadership style, and skills or passions. Many of these online inventories are extremely easy to use and have been surprisingly accurate. They scan much more than a person's potential giftedness, so we can see the person's entire ministry design that God has given him or her for service and ministry. However, the process does not end here.

An x-ray is useless if an employee is not there to interpret the results. So also is the process of identifying someone's ministry design without personal follow-up. This is the most important stage of integrating newcomers that most churches neglect. There must be a clear process to practically "scan" each person's life to effectively place him or her into the life of your congregation.

Every new person who completes our Connection Series schedules a forty-five-minute one-on-one conversation to discuss the results of his or her online inventory.

We are very clear that this is not an interview for a ministry or small-group position, but a way for us to help equip and release newcomers into existing groups. We use our findings to match them with a ministry that best fits their unique design, as well as a small group that best addresses their current needs in life (see example form).

Newcomers have been willing to share personal information with me, I feel, because our underlying goal is to strengthen, support, equip, and release them. It is for their benefit, not ours. I have discovered painful experiences, addictive pasts, and other struggles that would not have surfaced had I not spent the time to personally talk one-on-one.

Finding the Right Seat

The last stressor before flying is finding the seat that matches your ticket. Sometimes you find a seat next to the nicest person, and sometimes you find yourself sitting next to ... well you know what I mean. However, if you really do not like your seat, you can probably change it by asking a flight attendant.

We hold the same value with our integration process. Once the one-on-one discussions are complete, we meet as a pastoral staff to review each profile and recommend some "seats" for each newcomer. The overseeing pastor of the specific ministry or small group is then responsible for following up to personally invite each person to try it out for a period of time. Because the process is focused and clear, people feel free to try something else if our first suggestion is not a good fit.

Enjoying the Ride

Just like choosing a new vacation spot includes some risk, so does joining an established group. Keep the integration process clear, simple, personal, and most of all exciting. Let newcomers enjoy their journey as they travel on God's kingdom airlines.

Flexibility in Ministry

Dr. Doug Dees

If you are doing ministry but are not flexible, you may be doing over-organized religion. And if you are flexible, but are not doing ministry, you may just be involved in humanism. In both instances we miss God. Ministry that is flexible should depend on God. Flexibility within ministry must also depend on God. Since we are doing His work, we need to be willing to do what He wants, when He wants it, the way He wants it. Too much of the time we have structured ourselves to do ministry in certain ways at certain times. We define ourselves into a corner so that when He is looking for flexibility, we cannot be obedient. You have noticed already that this is not a section with a to-do list to follow. In this short treatise I want to simply get you thinking in a few new directions.

Is it possible that sometimes we define what ministry is in such narrow language that few people are able to do it? Does what you are attempting to do for Him have to be done on a certain day? Or in a certain way? Or at a certain time? Or by a certain person?

God seems to pick some odd people to do odd ministry in odd ways and at odd times. Moses was a stuttering murderer who did not really get started until age eighty. Paul persecuted Christians before becoming one and starting to witness almost immediately. Hosea was instructed to marry a prostitute. In Isaiah 20:3 Isaiah was instructed to walk naked for three years.

I am not suggesting we follow that example. But maybe we could allow God to be the one who directs our steps (Prov. 16:9).

If what we do is restricting what He wants, we could find ourselves working against God instead of with Him in His kingdom, no matter how great our intent is.

What Non-Flexibility Looks Like

On May 3, 1999, the strongest and most destructive tornado ever recorded chewed right through the middle of Moore, Oklahoma. It left a path thirty-eight miles long and a mile wide at many points. The path went right past the building belonging to the church I was serving as singles pastor. For a quarter mile across the street from the church building there was nothing left but rubble six feet deep. The National Guard commandeered our buildings as the central headquarters for all search and rescue operations. That evening the staff met to decide how we would proceed. There was no playbook for this one.

I remember one of the pastors telling us that we were going to have to be "flexible and positive." You cannot imagine how church life was disrupted. Our buildings and parking lot became the staging area to help the victims for miles around. We had tractor trailers loaded with supplies coming in by the hour. We had pallets of supplies stacked up and down our hallways. The new carpet we had put in recently was trashed. Displaced people lived in our buildings for weeks. The choir room was set up as a temporary morgue. We served thousands of meals from our kitchen. My office became the local insurance agent's office. Life at the church building was not the same. People and supplies were everywhere. It was chaos.

That Wednesday evening while we were frantically trying to get people helped and serving hundreds of meals to people still in their same clothes from two days ago. We were doing church that night instead of having our church's normal Wednesday night prayer meeting. Helping all those people was more important than our normal services, and we had to be flexible enough to see the need for shelter, food, and comfort that these people had.

In some instances ministry has been defined by a meeting at a certain time, in a certain building, done in a certain way—that ministry in the raw might not even be recognizable as ministry. I am not saying that our Wednesday night prayer meeting is not ministry. But if it is so narrowly defined that victims of a disaster cannot turn to the church to be flexible and to care for them, then we have lost sight of what ministry on Wednesday night should be. The words *ministry* and *deacon* translate forms of the Greek word diakonos, from the verb diakoneō that literally means "to serve." Ministry must include service. How much of the time are we involved in programs and positions in the church that have no impact? Too much I am afraid.

Leaders Set the Tone

When we as leaders desire to package what we do with our people in such narrowly defined ways, we cause inflexibility to happen. Make no mistake. If we are leading in this way, we are the problem. I wrote a book last year titled *ReSymbol*.[7] In it I explain how we have become "spiritual mimes." We just go through the motions. Mimes are odd things: they display lots of movement with nothing really happening.

In Ephesians 4 God has asked us to equip people. Sometimes we over-equip them in processes and programs, and never give them freedom to actually disciple others or allow them the freedom to discover what God has been asking them to do. As Acts 13:2 says, "The Holy Ghost said, Separate me Barnabas and Saul for the work whereunto I have called them," so must we allow the Holy Spirit to work today as He did then. It is possible that many times He is trying to work and we get in the way. A practical way to work this out in your church is this: as you plan, constantly remind yourselves that God can trump your plans. Tell Him you want to allow Him to do that. If you are too busy with your preplanned agenda items, you may not see God at work. Or perhaps you do see Him and cannot tear yourself away from your work to join Him in His.

Please do not think I am chastising you; I am not. I fight this problem daily. My to-do lists need to get done. But I am trying to get better at only putting items on my list that I feel He wants there. This is not a busywork list.

I have multiple lists. I try to support only systems and processes that are producing disciples. I try to make sure the systems and programs are invisible and the character of Christ is visible. But I also must allow Him to preempt my lists any time He wants.

People Vs. Programs

We must embrace that people are more important than programs or systems. I know we must have times and places to do ministry. We do not just wander the earth looking for needs; discipling takes persistence. Yet much of the time, our processes are overbearing and do not allow the personal side of Christianity to reign. It is interesting that Jesus took so much time to be with people. He never seemed to be rushed. He always stopped when someone had a need.

This is not rocket science; it is harder. You may be looking for a to-do list to counteract your inflexibility. Let me suggest that only one person, Christ, can do that. If, as we say, He is in control of our checkbook, then let Him and His Holy Spirit be in control of your time, your systems, and your programs. Let Him lead you.

Let me close by asking you a few questions to get your mind moving in a new direction. If your building burned to the ground and you could not rebuild, could you do church? Is your ministry defined by systems and programs? Or by helping people to look more like Jesus? Are your systems and programs producing disciples? If you could not order literature or meet regularly at a scheduled time, could you do church? How do you think it was possible for the early disciples, with no building, budgets, or printed materials, to turn the world upside down?

We sometimes define ministry too narrowly and we sometimes over-organize. We must make ministry something that is designed by and focused on Him. We must make sure that the ministry we already have going is Jesus centered. Otherwise we implement ideas and we focus on things that make it tough to be obedient to one of His last requests. What do you think Jesus meant when He said "go"? Are you flexible enough in ministry to obey?

Part Six
Motivation

Dealing with Burnout

Dr. Kevin Riggs

One Sunday morning a pastor friend of mine stepped behind the pulpit to deliver his weekly homily. It had been a normal Sunday. The choir sang, people made announcements, and church staff took an offering. My friend stood poised and opened his Bible to begin his sermon when something happened that shocked the entire congregation. He paused, as if searching for his prepared remarks, and then said, "I have had enough. I can't take it anymore. I quit." He then walked down the center aisle and out of the building, never to pastor again.

When I first heard about my friend, I felt sad and a little sorry. However, I must admit, there was a part of me that also felt admiration. A small part of me thought, "Wow. I wish I had the courage to do that." I dare say I am not alone. I bet a lot of church leaders have fantasized about telling the congregation how they really feel and then exiting the building.

I have no doubt what caused my friend to do what he did, and what caused me to think what I thought, was burnout. Burnout occurs when you are emotionally, spiritually, and physically exhausted as a result of pro-longed stress from feeling overwhelmed, under-capable, and unappreciated. Burnout is the job hazard of church leadership. Burnout reduces your productivity, saps your energy, and robs you of the joy and motivation that led you into ministry in the first place. Everyone has a bad day now and then; everyone periodically feels overwhelmed and underappreciated. But burnout is when you feel that way for a prolonged period of time.

Avoiding Burnout

The best way to deal with burnout is to avoid it at all costs. This is easier said than done, but there are some habits you can form in your life that will help keep burnout at bay. Here are just a few:

1. Set Margins

   Boundaries do not keep a person from enjoying life. Quite the contrary. Boundaries, or margins, give you freedom to enjoy and explore. Setting margins means you know your limitations. Do not serve on all committees. You cannot do everything, and God has not asked you to do everything. Setting margins means you learn what your strengths and weaknesses are, you learn to prioritize tasks, you learn to delegate, and you learn that the hidden word in the middle of burnout is *no*.

2. Exercise

   One of the best ways to avoid burnout is to exercise on a regular basis. Exercise improves blood flow to your brain. Much of the work church leaders do is mental. Intense thinking builds up toxic waste products, which

can result in fogginess. Something as simple
as a brisk walk can get the blood flowing
again, removing the toxic waste buildup in
your brain. Exercise also releases chemicals
(endorphins) into your bloodstream. These
chemicals give you a sense of happiness that
positively affect your overall attitude and
sense of well-being.

3. Eat a Balanced Diet

A balanced diet is key. Avoid extreme diet
programs. Talk to your doctor about eating a
healthy diet and drink plenty of good water.
Ingesting inadequate amounts of water, or
poor-quality water, can affect oxygenation of
the tissues.

4. Rest

One trait many church leaders share is their
continual violation of the commandment to
remember the Sabbath. The busiest day of the
week for church leaders is Sunday; if you do
not find time during the other days to rest,
you will burn out. The commandment to
remember the Sabbath is just as important as
the commandment to not commit adultery.

5. Observe Quiet Time

As church leaders it is easy to be so busy doing
ministry that we do not take time to refresh

and renew our own spirit. I cannot overstate the importance of developing and maintaining a regular and consistent time when you read the Bible (without thinking about sermons and lessons), pray, and journal.

6. Take Up Hobbies

   Do something different and unrelated to your church work. A change of pace gets your mind off your present circumstance onto something else. Your hobby could be golfing, biking, woodworking, gardening, or a host of other activities. A good hobby refreshes the spirit and gives you a new outlook on things.

7. Cultivate Relationships

   One of the greatest weapons to fight off burnout is a group of good friends—friends who love you for who you are, and friends who are not afraid to tell you when to slow down and take a break. You were not created to walk through life alone. Take the time to build a few close friendships.

Signs of Burnout (Physical, Emotional, Spiritual)

Since burnout affects every area of life, the signs of burnout surface in every area of life. Specifically, there are a host of physical, emotional, and spiritual signs of burnout. Here are just a few of them. (As you read, do not get hung up on the list. Some of the things listed could fall into a category other than burnout, and your list could be different from mine.)

1. Physical Signs

   Because prolonged stress depletes adrenal hormones in the body, you should expect burnout to affect a person physically. Prolonged fatigue may be the most common physical sign. The difference between burnout fatigue and simple exhaustion is that a good night's sleep usually makes the exhausted person feel better. But the body does not recover as quickly from fatigue when the fatigue is caused by prolonged stress. Other physical signs include a weakened immune system causing increased sickness and body aches, including, but not limited to, headaches, backaches, and muscle spasms.

2. Emotional Signs

   I think the main emotional sign of burnout is isolation. Oddly enough, when church leaders need people the most they avoid contact with others as much as possible. Isolation then leads to a lack of motivation, and no emotional energy to get anything accomplished. Another emotional sign of burnout is a lack of hope that things will ever change—a feeling that you will be forever stuck in your present circumstance. Two outward signs of emotional burnout are changes in sleeping patterns, either sleeping a lot or suffering through insomnia, and changes in appetite, either not eating at all (or very little) or eating all the time.

3. Spiritual Sign

   Lacking motivation and feeling tired all the time leads to neglecting your quiet time with God. Going days and weeks without reading the Bible, praying, and journaling opens the door for the enemy to attack the church leader. Satan really likes to kick you while you are down. Once your spiritual guard is down, feelings of being trapped in a hopeless situation creep in to your thought life. As a result, a burned-out minister begins to have self-doubt and feelings of failure. All of which ultimately lead to depression.

Recovering from Burnout

The good news is that burnout does not have to be terminal. Burnout can be overcome. How does a person recover from burnout? Here are a few suggestions:

1. Confess

   Nothing cures the soul like confession of

sins. Burnout, itself, may not be a sin, but the things that lead to burnout are. For example, pride causes a person to not ask for help. Pride convinces church leaders that we have all the answers and can work through any crisis. Confess this pride to God. Confess your tendency to be a people pleaser to Him. Confess these sins and others not only to God, but to someone you trust and someone who will pray for you.

2. Slow down

Remember God made the Sabbath for you (Mark 2:27). Learn to say no. Take regular, spiritual retreats.

3. Be Humble

Burnout could be God's way of reminding you that you are not God. You cannot do it all, you were not created to do it all, and God has not called you to do it all. Recognize where your strength comes from, and "walk humbly with thy God" (Mic. 6:8). God may have called you to be a church leader, but He has not called you to be Superman or Wonder Woman.

4. Be Accountable

If you do not share your struggles with someone, you will never really get beyond those struggles. Give someone in your life permission to ask you the tough questions and to let you know when you have overcommitted yourself and underdelivered to other people.

5. Goals and Priorities

Are your goals and priorities lined up with Scripture and with what you believe? Where does your family really fit in your goals and priorities? Are you serving to fulfill God's calling in your life or to be recognized by others? Only you can answer these questions.

Jesus told us His mission statement when He said that He came to "seek and to save that which was lost" (Luke 19:10). Saving is making something whole. To be lost, then, means to not be whole, or to be broken. Thus, Jesus came to put broken people back together again, making them whole. People, even church leaders, are broken physically, emotionally, and spiritually. All of Jesus' miracles had to do with healing people physically, emotionally, or spiritually. Jesus desires to make all church leaders physically, emotionally, and spiritually whole.

Passion and Enthusiasm
Kevin R. Scruggs

There are two events that will forever be etched in my memory. The first was when I was a child sitting at home with my family watching the 1980 Winter Olympics. The event was hockey. The match was between the United States and the Soviet Union. Due to my age I did not understand all of the dynamics that were involved, but I knew enough to know that we were the underdogs. As the game pressed on, my family became more and more engrossed in what we were watching. We cheered and yelled and cried as the seconds ticked down on the clock. When time had expired, you would have thought we had just won the lottery. USA! USA! USA! Those memories still give me goose bumps.

The second event was more recent; it was a few years ago when the New England Patriots were trying to finish a perfect season and they were playing the New York Giants in the Super Bowl. I am an Indianapolis Colts fan so I was not so much cheering for the Giants as I was cheering against New England. But you have to root for someone, right? It was near the end of the game, the Patriots had just scored and appeared to have the game won, especially since there was so little time left and they had so far to go for a touchdown. As the seconds wore on and play after play was completed, the impossible seemed possible, especially when the receiver caught the ball with his helmet.

When the Giants scored that improbable touchdown with almost no time left, I thought my lungs were going to explode. My family and I were screaming and cheering and giving high fives all over the room. I thought I had just witnessed the best Super Bowl ever. In those two moments, a group of people filled with passion and enthusiasm accomplished what seemed to be beyond believable. And the passion and enthusiasm that was on display spilled over and affected those of us who were fortunate enough to witness such an event. What if ministry was like that? What if we could be so engaged with what God has called us to do that our passion spilled over into other people's lives and encouraged them to do something too? I think it is possible, and I think it is what God wants us to do.

When you hear the words *passion* and *enthusiasm* you do not usually think about church. Most people think that serving God means a life of misery and discomfort. The key is showing them it is not that at all. You want to draw them in, not beg them to come in. Remember that attitude is contagious, whether good or bad.

Having passion and enthusiasm is important, but if it is not focused, you just waste energy. To start getting that energy on the correct path, you need to answer some fundamental questions. What am I passionate about? What is it that God is calling me to do? Write down your answers.

I realize that this may seem like a silly exercise, especially since you are already a congregational leader already excited about what you are doing, but people want to be a part of something greater than themselves. They are looking for a cause and for someone to lead them. If you do not have direction, you will have a difficult time keeping them with you.

Develop a plan for your passion. In any ministry there are many directions you can take and still get to the same destination. If someone else on your team has equal passion but wants to go a different direction, it is imperative to be able to articulate where you are headed. Otherwise you have the potential for disaster.

For example, let us say you are involved in missions and your passion is building relationships or teaching. Others may be thinking that since you are involved in missions you should have an evangelism program. Some may even be thinking that since your passion is in teaching and relationship building that perhaps you are in the wrong ministry altogether. What if you took your passion for teaching and building relationships and used it to train others in evangelism? What if you then took that same passion and went to a foreign country and helped a local missionary with your team? You knew what God had called you to do, you had a plan to use it, you drew others into that plan, and together you watched God do amazing things. Passion and enthusiasm are necessary, but without direction and purpose they can easily be wasted and lose effectiveness.

Ministry is a people-related endeavor. You, as one person, can realistically affect just a handful of people at one time. Remember that Jesus had only twelve disciples and of the twelve He heavily invested in a few. Once you realize what God has called you to do and have developed a plan, it is important for you to enlist the help of others. When you have like-minded people, your sphere of influence changes exponentially. Now your passion becomes their passion. Some of my fondest memories in ministry have been spent building relationships with leaders while we imagined the possibilities of what God was calling us to do. Take the time to invest in your fellow leaders. Celebrate and dream together. Working together spurs on creativity and lightens the load as you share leadership tasks.

No one can perform at 100 percent all of the time; it is impossible and it will lead to exhaustion or worse: resentment. It is a sad and difficult thing to watch a person go from passion to emptiness, but unfortunately it happens all too often. I was overseeing three different ministries that had me out on three different nights. We had volunteers who loved the ministry but I did not really give them much to do. All three ministries were growing slowly, which was starting to bug me. Maybe I just needed a little more effort. I went to a pastors' retreat where the speaker talked about pacing and said that if you were not careful your body would revolt. I actually laughed at his statement but a few weeks later I took two weeks of vacation.

During the vacation I began to feel sick, not physically, but emotionally. I was uncomfortable, irritable, and I knew something was wrong. On the way home from vacation I got the flu. Our original flight was full, so we took a different flight to another city and then had to rent a car to go back to the home airport to get our luggage. They lost mine. We went home to pick up our dog from the kennel, and that night she died. My life started spinning out of control. I was doing too much for too long, trying to run on my own, and now I could not do anything. The doctor diagnosed me with panic attacks and it took about six months to get them under control. I went from passion and enthusiasm to panic. God taught me a lot about pacing, about enlisting the help of others and bringing them along with me. Passion and enthusiasm are critical to having success in ministry and in life. God has put something in your heart; use it, and fan the flame.

God has called all of us to do something. You cannot invent passion and it is different for each one of us. When you find it, you know it. When you are operating within it, life seems effortless. If you have not found yours yet, do not worry. Begin by doing something you enjoy. God is a creative God. Perhaps what God has placed in your heart is something that is not even offered at your church. Yes, it may seem a little scary to step out on your own but do not worry; you are not on your own. There are others in your church just waiting for you to begin and they do not even know it. As they observe you using your giftedness, they will join you before you know it. That is the beauty of passion and enthusiasm. It is contagious.

Perseverance
Monty Waldron

Inviting you to explore the topic of perseverance is a lot like asking you to eat your vegetables. It is among those realities of the Christian life that we might be tempted to leave on the plate in favor of consuming more enjoyable provisions. There are so many other subjects that inspire us with flavors so much more immediately satisfying. But just like vegetables, perseverance is an essential part of a well-balanced meal—full of the nutrients we need for a vibrant walk with God. The less we know about and apply this vital topic, the harder it will be to finish well spiritually. In fact, that is the essence of perseverance: finishing well amid the hardships of living in a broken world.

Few phrases capture the heart of perseverance better than the words of Friedrich Nietzsche, later expounded upon by Eugene Peterson as the title of his book *A Long Obedience in the Same Direction*. If you have not read Peterson's book, it would be a great follow-up to this chapter. His assessment of Western Christianity is sobering: "Millions of people in our culture make decisions for Christ, but there is a dreadful attrition rate.... There is a great market for religious experience in our world; there is little enthusiasm for the patient acquisition of virtue."[8]

Growing spiritually is a challenge and there do not seem to be any shortcuts. Maturity comes only to those who stay the course through thick and thin over a long period of time, and that requires the all-important quality of perseverance. The apostles repeatedly list perseverance as an essential posture of those who long to experience faith, hope, and love to the fullest. It is to that end that I offer the following thoughts.

I have found it difficult to persevere when a spirit of entitlement governs my heart. The basis of that mindset is a belief that I know best what I need and when I need it. Why would I wait for God's timing and provision if I ultimately believe that my plan is better than His? Entitlement is accompanied by an acute awareness of what I do not have, and an equally acute lack of appreciation for what I do have. Numerous biblical illustrations show us that people experienced disastrous consequences as a result of taking matters into their own hands to get what they believed they deserved (Adam and Eve, Achan, King Saul, Judas, Ananias and Sapphira). In each case, God's best was lost by those who sought life outside of the boundaries God set for them.

Cultivate an Attitude of Gratitude

The only antidote I know for a spirit of entitlement is an attitude of gratitude. The more my focus remains on the immense goodness God has shown me spiritually and otherwise, the more content I am with my present circumstances. It does not mean that I never feel sad, angry, or lonely; it just means that my experience of a broken world is tempered by the love lavished on me in the midst of it. James teaches in his letter, "Every good gift and every perfect gift is from above, and cometh down from the Father of lights, with whom is no variableness, neither shadow of turning" (James 1:17). So I have endeavored to make it a practice of regularly reflecting on those things for which I am thankful. My wife and I have also sought to train our children in this by asking them to identify three things each night at bedtime for which they are thankful. After everyone has shared, we thank God together for His good gifts. The habit is helping us apply Paul's exhortation to "in every thing give thanks: for this is the will of God in Christ Jesus concerning you" (1 Thess. 5:18).

Be Honest Before God

Another key to cultivating perseverance is a heart commitment to honesty with God. The less I bring my struggles and disappointments to God in raw form, the less I am able to experience the compassion and care God has for me. The more distant I am from God's Fatherly love, the easier it is for me to lose heart. The enemy would like nothing more than for me to believe that God has left me to face life alone. When I choose to minimize or sanitize my thoughts and feelings with God, the more alone I begin to feel. I have heard it a hundred times, but it bears repeating: God is big enough to handle even the vilest stuff my heart can generate. I have found great solace in Jeremiah's words amid his anguish in Lamentations: "This I recall to my mind, therefore have I hope. It is of the LORD's mercies that we are not consumed, because his compassions fail not. They are new every morning: great is thy faithfulness" (Lam. 3:21–23).

Open Yourself to Others

In addition to bringing everything in my heart honestly to God, it is also important to open my heart to at least a couple of trusted friends. This is actually far more difficult for me than engaging God is. I became so self-reliant as a young person that I failed to learn the value of facing the hardships of life in authentic community. I learned to process everything internally and activate an external behavior that matched a righteous response. I am sure some of this was enabled by the Spirit, but I am also sure just as much was legalistic behavior management. I know this because I coddled "private" sins and justified them with a moral public persona. Sounds a little like the double-minded man described in James, does it not? It is a spiritually exhausting way to live; a surefire path to losing heart. The more I have learned to process my internal world in community (which is still a struggle at times), the more integrity I have experienced between my public and private life, and the more I have been able to persevere amid temptation and trial. It is indeed a trustworthy saying: "Two are better than one" (Eccl. 4:9). Or to say it another way, together is better.

Gain the Proper Perspective

Perseverance is not only about relationship; it is also about perspective. Our outlook on what constitutes life will dramatically affect our ability to remain steadfast for the long haul. If our view is limited primarily to the here and now, we will be blown around by the tyranny of the urgent and the allure of earthly desires. But if we widen our gaze to include all that is eternal, we will be capable of holding fast to the things that truly matter most: the glory of God and His redemptive plan. What a difference it would make if we would view our choices primarily in light of their eternal significance.

Eternity prioritizes things in ways that correct our natural inclinations. If left to ourselves, we will exchange our most precious possessions for cheap imitations that last only for a moment. How many marriages, ministries, friendships, and the like have been sacrificed at the altar of immediate gratification? C. S. Lewis says it beautifully:

> We are half-hearted creatures, fooling about with drink and sex and ambition when infinite joy is offered us, like an ignorant child who wants to go on making mud pies in a slum because he cannot imagine what is meant by the offer of a holiday at the sea. We are far too easily pleased.[9]

We are so because our perspective is stunted. We have bought into the lie that now is the best we can hope for. But true hope is found when we heed Paul's exhortation to "set your affection on things above, not on things on the earth" (Col. 3:2).

Easier said than done. Life is so full of demands, responsibilities, and distractions. As leaders, our days can be consumed with the immediate (and temporary) needs of the people we love and serve. How do we stay in touch with the present reality of the people we lead while focused on things above? That dilemma is the place where perseverance is most real for me. It is not just an interesting topic to write about, it is an essential way of life. And most surprising of all, it is not a choice to reach down deep and gut it out. Persevering as a leader is a tangible act of surrender. It is an acknowledgment that I will never be enough. The needs I encounter on a daily basis far exceed my ability and capacity.

The best thing I can do is to persevere in my personal relationship with Christ. This means that I cannot go without the daily discipline of renewing my mind with God's Word. I will never know enough of it to coast. This means that moments of solitude, reflection, and prayer are nonnegotiable. And the focus of this time needs to be on my own life and maturity. This also means that I am just as needy for God's grace and power as the congregation I lead. The moment I believe otherwise is the moment I begin to suffer the consequences of relying on the best of me without God. I have seen a number of phenomenal Christian leaders I have admired greatly unravel because they ceased to persevere in the careful cultivation of their own hearts toward God. Leaders who finish well are those who recognize that the best they have to offer is the fruit of God's faithful work in their own life. This, in my mind, is the essence of a long obedience in the same direction.

Encouragement and Affirmation

Kevin R. Scruggs

Ministry is hard. There, I said it. How is that for encouragement? It is hard to get up when you are feeling down, is it not? If you are reading this section of the manual, you are probably looking for some type of pick-me-up to either help you or to help you encourage others in ministry. There are times when we love doing ministry and then there are times when we would rather do anything other than ministry. The people, the politics of church, the needs—the problems seem to never end. I have to remind myself now and again that we live in a fallen world with lumpy bumpy people. There is always someone who needs you, something that needs to be done. How do you stay motivated?

Let me ask you something. How are you doing? Now before you answer I want you to know that I am not asking what you do, who you do it with, why you do it, or how well are you doing it. I just want to know how you are doing. This may be the first time anyone, yourself included, has asked you to answer that question genuinely in a very long time. So what is the answer? Let us say that you needed to scale it from one to ten, one being "questioning why I ever signed up for this" and ten being "this isn't work, this is paradise." Most of us fluctuate from one side to the other, but there are moments when we really do think about walking away and doing anything else! I believe that it is in those moments that God wants to speak into our lives the loudest.

Reflect

Do you remember when you became a church leader? Think back to when you knew this is what God called you to do. Take out a sheet of paper and on the top write: *What was it like in the beginning?* Think about it, remember what you loved, how God moved you, how much you enjoyed it all. Think about the ways God used you to affect lives. Recall these people's names, and faces, and memories. Write it down. We will come back to it in a few minutes. Also write down *How were you called to serve as a leader in your church?* Maybe you have never thought about that before. Everyone has a story, that moment when God places something in your heart that lets you know "this is what I am wired to do."

Recognize Your Role

One of my responsibilities in ministry has been to talk to people about their unique abilities. I explain that the church is a body and each member plays a specific role. The passage that comes to mind for most of us is found in 1 Corinthians 12:14, "For the body is not one member, but many." There are seasons of ministry when God calls us from one area to go serve in another. It is okay to make a change, but do not do it out of discouragement. I do not believe God desires that any of us become so riddled with guilt that we stay in one spot grinding it out until we die.

Realize That You Matter

Let us recap: you are serving as a leader in your church, you have recalled the exciting times when you first began this journey, and then you were reminded that you play a part in the bigger body. Are you with me? Great, so here is my question: what would your church be like without you? I am not kidding. What would it be like? I want to let you in on an important secret that the enemy does not want you to know or understand: you matter. If you do not believe me, read Psalm 139. Most churches do not say that its leaders matter for fear of egos running wild, but the fact still remains. If you were to stop doing what God has called you to do, it would have an impact on the church.

Two young brothers were walking along the beach together late one afternoon. The tide was rolling out and all over the beach were sand dollars drying out in the sun. There were hundreds of them. The younger brother began to stoop down and toss these little creatures back into the ocean, one by one. After a few minutes the older brother stopped the younger boy and said, "What are you doing? There are so many of them, you can't save them all. What does it matter?" The younger brother stood up with another sand dollar in his hand, looked at his brother, and said, "It matters to this one." And he threw the sand dollar back into the sea.

Let us go back to that list that I had you compile. Take a few moments and look at what you wrote down. Friend, there are times where we ask ourselves, "Why am I doing this? What difference am I making?" and we want to give up. Be encouraged because what you are doing matters to this One and to those lives He brings across your path. God has breathed into your heart a passion to serve His kingdom. You matter to Him and you are making a difference.

If I were to ask you where you are coming up short as a church leader, you could probably rattle off a list without too much trouble. Most of us are wired that way and at times we can be our own worst critic. It is often said that it takes three positive comments to offset one negative comment. We live in a world filled with armchair quarterbacks and Oprah experts; the church is no different.

Look to the Scriptures

So where do you get recharged? Where do you find encouragement? One of the places I like to go is my Bible. I am not trying to be "super spiritual"; I am trying to be practical. Psalm 18:19 tells us, "He brought me forth also into a large place; he delivered me, because he delighted in me." Did you know that God delights in you? This is one of my favorite verses in the Bible. God likes you and me. How is that for a positive comment?

It is easy to lose sight of how God really sees us. When I get discouraged, it can feel like God has abandoned me, that I have failed and He is disappointed. That is not God's heart; that is our enemy. God has promised to never leave us, never forsake us, especially when we feel all alone. If you find yourself feeling that way, talk to Him about it. God has big shoulders. He can handle it; plus it is not like He will be surprised by what you are saying. He is God, after all.

You Are Appreciated

Everybody needs encouragement, even you. Ministry is not easy but it is rewarding. So if you have not heard this in a while, thank-you for what you do. You are making a difference, even if you cannot see it right now.

There are many times in ministry when discouragement and criticism will try to creep in and, if we are not careful, we can get our eyes off of what God has called us to do. In those moments, remember that not only can God be trusted with your basic needs but He also wants to provide much more. Thank-you for faithfully serving the kingdom, and may God continue to use and bless what He has placed in your heart.

Endnotes

1. Preparation

1. Rusty Ricketson, *Follower First: Rethinking Leading in the Church* (Cumming, GA: Heartworks, 2009).

2. Ibid.

3. For further reading on the personal spiritual disciplines, see Donald S. Whitney, *Spiritual Disciplines for the Christian Life* (Colorado Springs: NavPress, 1991). To learn about the corporate spiritual disciplines, see Donald S. Whitney, *Spiritual Disciplines Within the Church* (Chicago: Moody, 1996).

4. Strategy

4. Richard Patterson, *Effectively Leading: A Guide for All Church Leaders* (Wheaton, IL: Evangelical Training Association, 1992).

5. Kenneth Gangel, *Biblical Leadership* (Wheaton, IL: Evangelical Training Association, 2006).

5. Problem Solving

6. English translations vary somewhat in the number of occurrences of the word *problem* (one to five times depending upon the English translation cited) but in the original languages of the Bible there are only two occurrences

(Deut. 1:12; Isa. 1:14) in the Old Testament and no occurrences in the New Testament.

7. Doug Dees, *ReSymbol* (Oviedo, FL: Higherlife Development Services, 2009).

6. Motivation

8. Eugene H. Peterson, *A Long Obedience in the Same Direction: Discipleship in an Instant Society*, 2nd rev. ed. (Downers Grove, IL: InterVarsity, 2000), 16.

9. C. S. Lewis, *The Weight of Glory: And Other Addresses* (New York: HarperCollins, 1949), 26.

Notes

Notes

Notes

Notes

Notes

Notes